Shared Watercourses and Water Security in South Asia

International Water Law

Volumes published in this Brill Research Perspectives title are listed at *brill.com/rpwl*

Shared Watercourses and Water Security in South Asia

Challenges of Negotiating and Enforcing Treaties

By

Salman M. A. Salman and Kishor Uprety

BRILL

LEIDEN | BOSTON

Originally published as Volume 3(3) 2018, in *International Water Law*, DOI:10.1163/23529369-12340011.

Library of Congress Control Number: 2018949172

Typeface for the Latin, Greek, and Cyrillic scripts: "Brill". See and download: brill.com/brill-typeface.

ISBN 978-90-04-38504-7 (paperback)
ISBN 978-90-04-38505-4 (e-book)

This journal is printed on acid-free paper and produced in a sustainable manner.

To the memory of Professor Charles B. Bourne (1921–2012); one of the pioneers and innovators in the field of international water law.

Contents

Acknowledgements

We would like to extend our sincere thanks and appreciation to Professor Gabriel Eckstein for undertaking the responsibilities of "Interim Editor-in-Chief" for this monograph, and for his efficient handling of the assignment. Our thanks and appreciation are also due to the other members of the Editorial Board of *Brill Research Perspectives in International Water Law* for their diligent overseeing of the process. The comments of the external reviewers, of Professor Eckstein, and the members of the Editorial Board have been quite helpful, and have improved the monograph considerably.

Shared Watercourses and Water Security in South Asia: Challenges of Negotiating and Enforcing Treaties

Salman M. A. Salman
Fellow, International Water Resources Association
Salmanmasalman@gmail.com

Kishor Uprety
International Lawyer and Researcher
Dr.kishoruprety@gmail.com

Abstract

Shared water resources have influenced South Asia's geography and history, as well as riparians' responses to the challenges of utilizing, managing, and protecting such resources. Because of scarcity, population growth, and climate change impacts on all the riparians, national calls for water security have become louder. Consequently, collaboration among the nations of South Asia for ensuring equitable sharing of such water resources has not been optimal. While most countries do not have reliable systems for data generation, those possessing some hydrological data consider them state secrets, restricting their exchange. Even when treaty obligations exist, data-sharing practices are *ad hoc*, and the range of information shared is limited. Thus, negotiating new transboundary water treaties amongst South Asia's riparian countries has become a daunting task, and enforcing existing ones remains a real challenge.

Keywords

Brahmaputra river – basin commissions – court of arbitration – Ganges river – Indus basin – UN watercourses convention

 | DOI:10.1163/9789004385054_002

Part 1: Introduction

1.1 *The Concept of Water Security*

The scarcity of water resources, their spatial and temporal variations, population growth and urbanization, climate change and environmental degradation, and the sharing of many watercourses by two or more states, have given a steady rise to competing demands over shared water resources among riparians. This situation, *inter alia*, has led to the emergence of the concept of water security, stressed by many governments around the globe, particularly in South Asia; each country for itself and its own population.

Indeed, for individual riparian states, water has become a major, if not the main, part of their national security priorities, and their perceived resolution lies in securing as much water as possible for their citizens. This resolution tends to give lower priority to regional cooperation, and instead, to concentrate on maximum national uses of water, which often result in unsustainable patterns of consumption and increased risks for poor management, as well as disputes amongst riparians. In that midst, a subtle divide has also emerged, largely between national water security concerns and actions on the one hand, and the international legal regime for shared watercourses on the other. As a result, concerns and actions of nations around the globe with regard to their water security frequently, if not always, clash with the international legal regime for governance of transboundary watercourses.

Traditionally, water security had two meanings which apply to both the rights of an individual and to the claims of a state on behalf of its citizen. The traditional meaning of water security centered around a physically dependable supply, which can be tied to a legal allocation, or it can be simply based on capture, and a low risk that any other party can interfere with the capture. Because of increasing uncertainty about future supplies of water, the concept of water security today is being expanded beyond these traditional definitions to include the guarantee of sufficient water for a nation's sustainable food production. The assumption is that unless sufficient water exists for this and other related health purposes, the lack of adequate water will become a source of social insecurity, or even violence.[1]

1 For a detailed discussion of these issues, *see*, A. D. Tarlock, '*Water Security, Fear Mitigation and International Water Law*', 31(3) Hamlin Law Review (2008) 703–728, at 724–725. Literature review portrays differing and divergent views on those issues of water security; *see* C. Leb & P. Wouters, '*The Water Security Paradox and International Law: Securitization as an Obstacle to Achieving Water Security and the Role of Law in Desecuritizing the World's Most Precious Resources*', in B. Lankford et al. (eds.), *Water Security: Principles, Perspectives, and Practices*

1.1.1 The Global Spread of the Concept

The Organisation for Economic Co-operation and Development has classified water security as a 'major policy challenge confronting governments around the world.'[2] This challenge comprises managing risks of water shortages, water excesses and floods, and inadequate water quality, as well as the risk of undermining the resilience of freshwater systems.

Indeed, unmanaged risks in one river basin can pose enormous challenges not just for the individual riparian states regionally, but for other vested national and sub-national security interests as well as globally. The study, *Global Water Security*, launched at the 2012 World Water Day,[3] presented the concerns regarding water availability in certain transboundary rivers (particularly the Jordan, the Nile, and the Indus) as a development that will impact national security interests for the United States of America itself. The report also indicated that North Africa, the Middle East, and South Asia 'will face major challenges coping with water problems' due to 'demographic and economic development pressures.'[4] The report clearly places water security at the top of the agenda of national security, thereby linking water security, both national and global, with transboundary water governance.[5] This is the reality each region or group of riparians needs to consider, and grapple with, while developing the international legal regime for its shared water resources.

It is important to stress, at this point, that the concept of 'water security' which was an abstract notion until recently, has gradually gained the status of a valid and definable concept.[6] Yet, it is very much a political, not a legal concept. Indeed, in legal and practical terms, it is extremely difficult to define

---

(London: Routledge, 2013) 26–45; *see also* T. Kuokkanen, '*Water Security and International Law*', PER/PELJ 2017 (20), http://www.scielo.org.za/pdf/pelj/v20n1/08.pdf.

2 Organisation for Economic Co-operation and Development, '*Water Security for Better Lives*', OECD Studies on Water (Paris: OECD Publishing, 2013) at 11, https://www.oecd.org/env/resources/Water%20Security%20for%20Better%20Lives-%20brochure.pdf.

3 Intelligence Community Assessment, '*Global Water Security*', ICA 2012–08, U.S. Office of the Director of National Intelligence (2 February 2012), https://www.dni.gov/files/documents/Special%20Report_ICA%20Global%20Water%20Security.pdf.

4 *See id.*, at 1.

5 *See* generally, D. D. Raman, *Governance of International Rivers: Threats, Gaps and Challenges* (Unpublished Ph. D. Thesis, University of Waikato, 2015).

6 It is worth adding in this context that 'The Hague Ministerial Declaration', issued at the end of the Second World Water Forum on March 22, 2000, is entitled 'Water Security in the 21st Century'. The Hague Declaration spelt out the concept of water security as no more than an aspiration when it stated in the opening paragraph 'business as usual is not an option. There is, of course, a huge diversity of needs and situations around the globe, but together we have one common goal: to provide water security in the 21st Century.' Thus, the Declaration dealt with water security in the political and socio-economic, but not the legal, contexts. Moreover,

or implement the concept simply because the concept has different connotations among its proponents, globally, regionally, nationally, and locally.[7] Also, as mentioned above, water security of one country would, in most instances, clash with the water security of other countries sharing the same watercourse because of the limited amount of water in that watercourse.

1.1.2 Challenges of Operationalizing the Concept

As discussed above, there are clear difficulties with, and challenges to, the concept of water security. These difficulties surfaced abundantly during the negotiations, for instance, of the Nile Basin Cooperative Framework Agreement (CFA).[8] The negotiations which commenced under the auspices of the Nile Basin Initiative (NBI) in 1999,[9] and lasted for more than ten years, ran into major differences over the sharing of the Nile waters between the two

---

as a declaration, it has no legally-binding effect. The Hague Ministerial Declaration is available at: http://www.cbd.int/doc/handbook/cbd-hb-11-en.pdf.

7 For an interesting discussion of the concept of water security, *see* generally, P. Wouters et al., '*Water Security, Hydrosolidarity, and International Law: A River Runs Through It*', Yearbook of International Environmental Law (2009) 97–135. As per these authors, the notion of security, and water security in particular can have different meanings and acquire various forms (at the individual, local, national, regional, and global levels). However, the authors point out that at the regional or national basin level, the water security challenges have manifested themselves most visibly, and the international legal response has been particularly pronounced. The authors argue that the evolving international legal frameworks that govern transboundary water resources provide an appropriate platform for addressing water security concerns. The notions of equity, reasonableness, fairness, and sustainability, which are enshrined as the key principles of international water law, properly reflect the core objectives of the fair and effective management of the world's shared water resources, and thus of the promotion of regional and global peace and security; *see id.* at 98. However, UN-Water defined 'water security' in a different way, emphasizing the role of the population and not that of the state. UN-Water defined water security to mean '[t]he capacity of a population to safeguard sustainable access to adequate quantities of acceptable quality water for sustaining livelihoods, human well-being, and socio-economic development, for ensuring protection against water-borne pollution and water-related disasters, and for preserving ecosystems in a climate of peace and political stability.' *See* '*What is Water Security? Infographic*', UN Water, (2013), http://www.unwater.org/publications/water-security-infographic/.

8 The Nile Basin Cooperative Framework Agreement 2010 (CFA) is available at: http://www.nilebasin.org/images/docs/CFA%20-%20English%20%20FrenchVersion.pdf.

9 The Nile Basin Initiative (NBI) was officially born 22 February 1999 in Dar-es-Salam, Tanzania. In a meeting, the ministers of water resources of nine Nile riparian countries signed the minutes establishing the NBI as an inter-governmental organization and as a transitional arrangement to foster cooperation and sustainable development of the Nile River, for the benefit of the inhabitants of those countries. *See* Nile Basin Initiative website at http://www.nilebasin.org/newsite/.

lower riparians (Sudan and Egypt) and the remaining upper riparian countries. Such differences centered around the application and interpretation by each of these two groups of Nile riparians of the principles of equitable and reasonable utilization and the obligation against causing significant harm, and the question as to which of the two principles supersedes the other. The differences arose despite the wide global acknowledgement that the obligation not to cause significant harm is, indeed, subordinate to the principle of equitable utilization.[10]

Egypt and Sudan claimed two contested treaties of 1902 and 1929 were valid (usually referred to as the colonial treaties),[11] alleging that the two treaties give them power to veto projects on the Nile in the upper riparian countries,[12] and thus, protect their acquired uses and rights against any harm by the upper

10 For a detailed discussion of this issue, *see* S. McCaffrey, *The Law of International Watercourses* (2nd ed., Oxford: Oxford University Press, 2007); C. Bourne, '*The International Law Association's Contribution to International Water Resources Law*', 36 Natural Resources Journal (1996) 155–216. *See also* S. M. A. Salman, '*Entry into Force of the UN Watercourses Convention—Why Should It Matter?*', 31:1 International Journal of Water Resources Development (2015) 4–16. *See also* the decision of the International Court of Justice (ICJ) in the *Gabčíkovo-Nagymaros Case* (ICJ, *Case concerning the Gabčíkovo-Nagymaros Project, Hungary v. Slovakia*), Judgement, 25 September 1997, http://www.icj-cij.org/files/case-related/92/092-19970925-JUD-01-00-EN.pdf. In that case, the ICJ emphasized the principle of equitable and reasonable utilization when it directed that 'the multi-purpose programme, in the form of a coordinated single unit, for the use, development and protection of the watercourse is implemented in an equitable and reasonable manner.' The ICJ did not refer to the obligation not to cause harm. The ICJ endorsed and underscored the principle again in 2010 in the *Pulp Mills Case* between Argentina and Uruguay (ICJ, *Case concerning Pulp Mills on the River Uruguay (Argentina v. Uruguay)*, Judgement, 10 April 2010, http://www.icj-cij.org/files/case-related/135/135-20100420-JUD-01-00-EN.pdf.

11 The 1902 treaties Between United Kingdom and Ethiopia and Between the United Kingdom, Italy and Ethiopia relative to the Frontiers between the Soudan, Ethiopia and Eritrea, (Addis Ababa, May 15, 1902, Treaty Series No.16 (1002) (Printed for His Majesty's Stationery Office, London, www.treaties.fco.gov.uk (visited May 27, 2018), and the 1929 Treaty (Great Britain and Northern Ireland and Egypt, Exchange of Notes in regard to the Use of the Waters of the River Nile for Irrigation Purposes. Cairo, May 7, 1929, League of Nations Treaty Series, Volume 93–94: 1929).

12 Egypt claims to have succeeded to the 1902 treaty between Britain and Ethiopia, and alleges further that the treaty gives it veto power over projects on the Nile in Ethiopia: a claim rejected totally by Ethiopia. Egypt also claims that the 1929 treaty between Britain (on behalf of its colonies of Kenya, Tanganyika, Uganda, and Sudan) and Egypt gives it veto power over projects on the Nile in these British colonies. In contrast, Kenya, Tanganyika (now Tanzania), and Uganda claim that the agreement does not bind them anymore. For a thorough discussion of these issues *see* S. M. A. Salman, '*The Changing Legal Contours of the Nile Basin: Do Agreements Really Matter?*', in S. McCaffrey et al. (eds.), *Research Handbook on International Water Law* (Cheltenham: Edward Elgar, 2018, forthcoming).

riparians. The validity of these treaties, as well as the claims of Egypt and Sudan, were totally rejected by the upper riparians. As the differences persisted, the facilitators and negotiators decided to introduce the concept of water security in the CFA, hoping that the concept could break the deadlock.[13]

Article 2 of the CFA defines water security as 'the right of all Nile Basin States to a reliable access to and use of the Nile River system for health, agriculture, livelihoods, production, and environment.' Further, Article 14 of the CFA, titled 'Water Security', reads:

> Having due regard to the provisions of Articles 4 and 5, Nile Basin States recognize the vital importance of water security to each of them. The States also recognize that the cooperation, management, and development of the waters of the Nile River System will facilitate achievement of water security and other benefits. Nile Basin States therefore agree, in a spirit of cooperation to work together to ensure that all states achieve and sustain water security.

In a unique and unprecedented fashion, the CFA left a blank paragraph (14(b)), clarifying in a footnote that the unresolved Article 14(b) was attached to the agreement to be resolved by the Nile River Basin Commission within six months of its establishment.

It is worth recalling that Articles 4 and 5 of the CFA deal, respectively, with the principle of equitable and reasonable utilization, and the obligation against causing significant harm. The cross-reference to Articles 4 and 5, thus, confirms that the linkages between the two principles and the concept of water security were clearly on the minds of the negotiators.

All the Nile upper riparian countries participating in the negotiations (Burundi, Democratic Republic of Congo, Ethiopia, Kenya, Rwanda, Tanzania and Uganda), therefore, agreed to this proposal. However, the two lower riparians, Egypt and Sudan, rejected it. They demanded and insisted that Article 14 of the CFA should include a specific provision, obligating the basin states 'not to adversely affect the water security and current uses and rights of any other Nile Basin State.'[14] Hence, without solving any problem, the introduction of the concept of water security reopened the major pre-NBI differences over

---

13 *See* D. Z. Mekonnen, '*The Nile Basin Cooperative Framework Agreement Negotiations and the Adoption of a "Water Security" Paradigm: Flight into Obscurity or a Logical Cul-de-sac?*: 21:2 European Journal of International Law (2010) 421–440.

14 CFA, supra note 8, art. 14.

the Nile colonial treaties and existing uses and rights,[15] and derailed the CFA negotiations process, resulting in failure to reach the very inclusive treaty the facilitators and negotiators set themselves to achieve.[16]

It is worth adding that the concept of water security does not exist in any multilateral or bilateral water treaty. Also, as already noted above, it does not have a status of universally recognized legal theory; it is merely a political and socio-economic concept.

1.1.3 Theorizing Water Security in South Asia

In the South Asian context (defined in this monograph to include the seven countries of Afghanistan, Bangladesh, Bhutan, China, India, Nepal, and Pakistan), more specifically, national water security attempts to deal broadly with risks associated with household, economic, urban and environmental securities, resulting in intense pressure on shared river basins. It has taken an urgent and significant place in their concerns, agenda and actions.

With less than 20% of the total global water availability, about 40% of the world population of 7.5 billion in 2017 (close to three billion people) live in these seven countries. Their annual population growth, averaging close to 1.5%, is one of the highest in the world.[17] Fast moving industrialization and urbanization, particularly in China and India, and environmental degradation everywhere pose major threats to their water resources. Climate change, represented by the increased frequency of droughts and accelerated melting of Himalayan glaciers, further exacerbate their dire water resources situation.

The seven countries of South Asia share a large number of rivers, but have not succeeded in concluding a single agreement including all the riparians on any river. Moreover, the few agreements concluded, thus far, face major difficulties with their interpretation and implementation; negotiation of new agreements suffer from the daunting challenge of reluctance, if not outright failure, of the states to share hydrological data and information and an absence of trust and good faith.

A report by the Asia Foundation described South Asia's transboundary water management and cooperation as highly nationalistic, technocratic, and zealously securitized. It stated that in Bangladesh, India, Nepal, and Pakistan, data on the selected rivers are collected and held by government departments

---

15 *See* generally Salman, *The Changing Legal Contours of the Nile Basin*, supra note 12.

16 *See* S. M. A. Salman, *'The Nile Basin Cooperative Framework Agreement: A Peacefully Unfolding African Spring?'*, 38:1 Water International (2013) 17–29 at 17.

17 World Bank, *World Development Indicators* (Washington, DC, 2017), https://data.worldbank.org/data-catalog/world-development-indicators (visited 10 January 2018).

in a fragmented manner and are not systematically collected at a basin level. The report further indicated that water information is shared more informally piecemeal between countries having better relations.[18] Each country has been moving in the direction of planning and executing its unilateral development plans, supposedly to counter the competing demands of other riparians. This, in turn, has propelled the concept of water security in South Asia to prominence. The report basically highlights the water security approach by each of the seven countries of South Asia.

1.2 *The Geopolitical Setting of South Asia's Shared Watercourses*

The seven countries of South Asia dealt with in this monograph are drained by nearly 20 major Himalayan rivers broadly belonging to three sub-regions. The Western sub-region includes the Indus system to which the Jhelum, Chenab, Ravi, Beas, and Sutlej Rivers belong, with India, Pakistan, China, and Afghanistan as riparians. The Central sub-region includes the Ganges system to which the Yamuna, Ramganga, Mahakali, Karnali, Gandaki, and Kosi Rivers belong, with India, Bangladesh, Nepal, and China as riparians. The Eastern sub-region includes the Brahmaputra system to which the Teesta, Raidak and Manas Rivers belong, with India, Bangladesh, Bhutan, and China as riparians. Several other tributaries of these rivers also flow through more than one country, and thus fall into the category of international rivers. India is at the center (geographically) of all these countries and basins.[19]

The two basic characteristics of water resources that significantly influence the hydro-behavior of the countries in South Asia are floods and drought. Much of the annual precipitation takes place during the monsoon season (June to

18 *See* M. Surie & S. Prasai, *Strengthening Transparency and Access to Information on Transboundary Rivers in South Asia* (New Delhi: The Asia Foundation, March 2015).

19 One author noted that the transboundary water sharing issues in South Asia are primarily Indo-centric, naturally due to India's geographical location and its size. The author added that India seems to be in the middle of all transboundary water sharing disputes, and its status as the regional hegemon and its influence over her smaller neighbors, except for Pakistan, seem to constitute the core of the water sharing disputes. *See* N. Kadurugamuwa, *Sharing of Trans-Boundary River Waters in South Asia; Geopolitics and Beyond* (2014) at 96. It is noteworthy that India is the upper riparian of the transboundary river systems in South Asia except in the case of Nepal and China. Another author noted that due to the dominant position India takes by virtue of size, population, growth potential, economic and technological capacities, stable political system, and the upstream position it has in the main rivers, it could be said that India is *the designated country to take the hegemonic position* (italics added for emphasis). *See also* J. C. Keetelaar, *Transboundary Water Issues in South Asia* (MSc Thesis, Erasmus University Rotterdam, International Public Management & Policy, 2017) at 21.

September) and inundates large areas of the region. During the dry months, the flows of the rivers, being at their lowest levels, increase the possibility for drought. Freshwater resources per capita, indicating a major variation amongst countries, as well as amongst regions within the same country, puts continual and tremendous pressure on the available resources, leading to an increase in the competing demands for the waters of the international rivers. This in turn has led to, and dictated the construction of dams to harness and ensure water and power availability and security.[20] However, the dozens of dams, whether on the Indus, the Ganges, or the Brahmaputra basin rivers, existing, planned or projected, are considered threats by the other riparians, upper and lower alike. Indeed, these dams are unilateral development projects, with no joint planning, construction, financing, management or use. Upstream users cite vital developmental imperatives to justify such construction, while downstream riparians oppose them by citing their existing uses that depend on the flows. This dilemma, caused by divergent views, underscores and heightens the level of lack of cooperation, as well as perceived and real threats, and calls for the establishment and strengthening of transboundary arrangements, not only for sharing water and ensuring governance, but also preventing conflict.[21] However, any movement in this direction necessitates crafting of water treaties that are in full cognizance of international water law. This is a daunting task, as will be discussed in some detail in this monograph.

1.3 *Roadmap of the Monograph*

Against this background, this monograph discusses the legal regimes and arrangements pertaining to transboundary waters established by the countries of South Asia in their attempts to arrive at a fair allocation of their shared watercourses. It first provides an analytical overview of the treaty regimes and then discusses the various challenges of treaty negotiations, implementation, and enforcement faced by these countries, which leads to their inability to harness optimal benefits pertaining to water and power. The monograph also attempts, wherever relevant, to compare or relate the provisions of the treaties

20 *See* generally, B. Chellaney, 'From Arms Racing to "Dam Racing" in Asia, How to Contain the Geopolitical Risks of the Dam-Building Competition,' Paper Series, *Transatlantic Academy* (May 2012) at 3, http://www.transatlanticacademy.org/publications/arms-racing-dam-racing-asia-how-contain-geopolitical-risks-dam-building-competition.

21 For an analysis of this matter, *see* B. Chellaney, *Water: Asia's New Battleground* (Washington, DC: Georgetown University Press, 2011); *see also* K. Uprety, '*South Asian Water Treaty Practice: An Overview*', in S. McCaffrey et al. (eds.), *Research Handbook on International Water Law* (Cheltenham: Edward Elgar, 2018, forthcoming), Chapter 25.

with international water law to help analyze and understand the areas of convergence and divergence.

In this context, the monograph argues that the challenges for ensuring fair and optimal water sharing arrangements in South Asia are related mainly to political mistrust amongst riparian countries (leading to difficulties in exploring and negotiating treaties), political asymmetry,[22] divergent national water ethos and approaches manifested in the adoption of the concept of water security, and imbalance in supply and demand. The challenges also relate to weak understanding of international water law (leading to difficulties in executing its principles) and fragile internal political governance (leading to inefficiency in garnering stakeholder support in enforcing treaty obligations). The monograph concludes with some thoughts and suggestions to assist the countries of South Asia in moving forward with optimal, sustainable, and beneficial utilization of their shared watercourses.

Part 2: South Asia's Treaty Practice on Shared Watercourses

As noted above, the focus of the countries of South Asia has been to ensure water security for people in a situation of constant scarcity, resulting in competing demands and variability in access. However, notwithstanding the critical nature and status of water resources in the livelihood of their people, these South Asian countries have not succeeded in establishing treaty regimes for sharing the waters of most of their international rivers. Only a handful of treaties have been concluded by some of the riparian countries, and not without serious political and diplomatic difficulties. Indeed, none of these treaties is inclusive of all the riparians to any shared watercourse. The Indus Waters Treaty between India and Pakistan; a series of treaties on the Ganges River between India and Bangladesh; and the Kosi, the Gandak and the Mahakali treaties between India and Nepal are specific examples. All these treaties are

22 For discussion of these issues, *see* K. B. Malla, *The Legal Regime of International Watercourse Progress and Paradigms Regarding Uses and Environmental Protection* (Ph.D. dissertation, Stockholm University, Faculty of Law, 2005), particularly, Chapter 5 on Asian Rivers (at 135–164) and Chapter 11 on Himalayan Water Basin (at 259–303); *see also* J. S. Mehta, '*Politics of Riparian Relations. Sustaining Development and Peace*', in B. G. Verghese & R. R. Iyer (eds.), *Harnessing the Eastern Himalayan Rivers: Regional Cooperation in South Asia* (New Delhi: Konark, 1994) 159–172; B. G. Verghese, '*The Indo-Bhutan, Indo-Nepal Dialogues*', in *id.*, 199–211.

bilateral, and none of these countries has entered any water sharing agreement with China on any of the rivers that originate there.[23] Nor is there any treaty between Pakistan and Afghanistan on the Kabul River, a major tributary of the Indus, which flows through Afghanistan and joins the Indus in Pakistan.[24] Apart from the legal regimes already established by the above treaties, there are also a few regimes that are under development, as will be discussed in Part 2.2 of this monograph.

2.1 *Regimes for Shared Watercourses in Force*

2.1.1 The Indus River System

The Indus River originates in Tibet near Lake Manasarovar, the highest freshwater lake in the world (15,000 feet). The River initially flows northwest for 600 miles, and then turns south, draining the high mountains of India. It then flows through Pakistan before emptying into the Arabian Sea, southeast of Karachi. The Indus River system consists of the main stem Indus and five major tributaries, all of which flow through India before reaching Pakistan. They collectively make up one of the largest natural irrigation channels in the

---

23 China is also a country that shares a considerable number of international watercourses, some of which are of global significance. Rather than adopt a multilateral strategy, China has chosen to sign several bilateral treaties with its neighboring countries concerning its international watercourses. *See* H. Chen, '*The 1997 UNWC and China's Treaty Practice on Transboundary Waters*', http://www.unwatercoursesconvention.org/images/2012/10/China-and-UNWC-Study.doc. As pointed out by Chen, most of the current transboundary water treaties are related to the waters in the north-east and north-west areas, with very few in the south-west area. Most of these treaties are bilateral, taking the model of one-country-one-treaty, rather than one-river-one-treaty. The UN Watercourses Convention has some impact and relevance in China's treaty practice notwithstanding the fact that China voted against the Convention, as will be discussed later; *see id. See also* generally, H. Chen et al., '*Exploring China's Transboundary Water Treaty Practice Through the Prism of the UN Watercourses Convention*', 38:2 Water International (2013) 217–230.

24 The few treaties concluded by China on its shared water resources are worth taking note of because water policies of one country do affect other riparians; and bigger countries' policies affect even more. India's policy and practice of dealing with riparians, for instance, affect three river systems (the Ganges, Brahmaputra and Indus). Similarly, China's riparian policy affects nine countries of the south, on five river systems, the Indus, the Ganges, the Brahmaputra, the Salween and the Mekong. *See* G. Siwakoti, *Transboundary River Basins in South Asia: Options for Conflict Resolution* (Berkeley: International Rivers, 2011), https://www.internationalrivers.org/sites/default/files/attached-files/transboundary riverbasins.pdf.

world.[25] India is the upper riparian nation on virtually every tributary of significance in the basin, except for the Kabul River.[26]

The Indus flows are highly variable and depend on summer monsoons and the Himalaya's melting snow. With about 70% of the total annual runoff occurring between June and September, it is one of the largest sediment-producing rivers in the world. It is also the most important water source for irrigated agriculture, primarily for Pakistan, and a significant source of power generation for both Pakistan and India. In the 1850s, the British East India Company built a complex system of canals to move water in what was then India.[27] The system was later enhanced by the construction of extensive diversion structures and canals in Pakistan, now commonly referred to as the Indus Basin Irrigation System.[28]

---

25 The Indus Basin countries include Pakistan (52%), India (34%), Tibet/China (7%), Afghanistan (6%), Disputed (China/India) (<1%), and Nepal (<1%). *See* United Nations Environment Programme, *Atlas of International Freshwater Agreements* (2002) at 63, http://wedocs.unep.org/handle/20.500.11822/8182.

26 Afghanistan is endowed with three major river basins: Amu Darya (Amu Darya Basin), Helmand (Sistan Basin) and Kabul (Indus Basin). The utilization of waters from the Helmand, which flows from Afghanistan to Iran, had long poisoned relations between Iran and Afghanistan. Indeed, the Helmand River had been the source of contention since the late 1800s. In the nineteen and early twentieth centuries, British assistance was sought primarily by Iran in the arbitration of the dispute over Helmand River waters, but by the 1950s, for geopolitical and aid-related reasons, it was the United States who was appealed to for international advice. The US assistance expanded to form a fact-finding commission, which made a series of recommendations in 1951. Iranian-Afghan parleys on the subject were resumed in June 1972, and culminated in the Helmand River Water Treaty of 13 March 1973 (revised 6 June 1977), thus ending the century-old conflict. Iran's approach to this treaty was based on the idea that international relations are more important than the development of the region, and therefore it evinced a spirit of accommodation and conciliation. Another agreement for the utilization of the Helmand River waters was signed in 2002. *See* A. Lamballe, *L'Eau en Asie du Sud. Confrontation ou Coopération?* (Harmattan 2009) at 63. The Helmand Treaty is the only Afghan instrument that deals with water allocations for that country. *See* for some discussion, G. Hearns, '*The Helmand River and the Afghan-Iranian Treaty 1973*', International Water Law Project Blog (23 July 2015), https://www.internationalwaterlaw.org/blog/2015/07/23/the-helmand-river-and-the-afghan-iranian-treaty-of-1973/.

27 C. D. Thatte, '*Indus Waters and the 1960 Treaty Between India and Pakistan*', in O. Varis et al. (eds.), *Management of Transboundary Rivers and Lakes* (Berlin and Heidelberg: Springer, 2008) 165–206, at 176.

28 Major reservoir projects include the Tarbela (Pakistan–Indus), the Bhakra-Nangal (India–Sutlej), the Pong (India–Beas), the Mangla (Pakistan–Jhelum), and the Nathpa–Jhakri (India–Sutlej); compiled from data *available at*: http://www.wapda.gov.pk. *See also* J. Briscoe & U. Qamar et al., 'Pakistan's Water Economy: Running Dry', Country Water Resources Assistance Strategy Report 44375, *World Bank* (2006).

2.1.1.1 *Road to the Indus Waters Treaty*

The road to the Indus Waters Treaty was long and turbulent. When Pakistan was established in 1947, as a result of the partitioning of India,[29] the topography and existing irrigation infrastructure on the Indus River were largely ignored. The canal system built for irrigating the huge lands of the scheme was divided between the two countries to meet a political compromise. The practical consequence of this act was more portentous than the political tragedy. As a result, 80% of the land irrigated by the Indus River and its tributaries became part of Pakistan, but the headwaters of the entire Indus River system remained in India. Partition literally divided a set of canals between the West Punjab (Pakistan) and the East Punjab (India), with India receiving control of upstream rivers that supplied water to both West and East Punjab.[30]

Consequently, the Indus River became a source of tension between the two nations within weeks of Pakistan's establishment. In 1948, India closed the canals in its territory on two rivers (Ravi and Sutlej), cutting off Pakistan's supply of water to irrigate lands in the West Punjab. A month later, it re-opened the canals as part of an Inter-Dominion Agreement, but asserted its right to control the entire water supply of the Ravi, Sutlej, and Beas Rivers.[31]

In view of the increasing tension, both countries, along with the international community, felt the urgency for a sharing framework of the Indus waters; hence negotiations resumed in earnest under the auspices of the good offices of the World Bank.[32] After close to ten years of negotiations, India and Pakistan

---

29 The British Parliament approved the Partition plan on 18 July 1947, but the boundaries delineation took place later.

30 *See* S. M. A. Salman & K. Uprety, *Conflict and Cooperation on South Asia's International Rivers: A Legal Perspective* (The Hague: Kluwer Law International, 2003; Washington, DC: The World Bank, 2003) at 41.

31 *Inter-Dominion Agreement Between the Government of India and the Government of Pakistan*, India-Pakistan, 4 May 1948, http://www.internationalwaterlaw.org/regional-docs/punjab-canal.html. India claimed that the proprietary rights in those waters vested wholly in the East Punjab government, and that the West Punjab government could not claim any share of those waters as a right; a claim forcefully disputed by Pakistan. As such, it is theoretically debatable as to whether India asserted the 'Harmon Doctrine' but, no doubt, its claim of its rights was unequivocal. *See also* Uprety, *South Asian Water Treaty Practice*, supra note 21.

32 David Lilienthal, former Chairman of the Tennessee Valley Authority, wrote an article making a series of recommendations pertaining to the Indus system of rivers, following his visit to the region. The recommendations included, *inter alia*, that the Indus Basin be managed and developed as a single unit; that financing be provided by India, Pakistan, and the World Bank; and that the Indus be administered by an Indo-Pakistan mixed body or a multinational body. Eugene Black, the President of the World Bank at the time, acquiesced to Lilienthal's recommendations and decided to react positively to the opportunity.

signed the Indus Waters Treaty on 19 September, 1960,[33] with the World Bank as a third-party signatory for certain purposes that were spelt out clearly in the Treaty.[34]

2.1.1.2 *Salient Features of the Indus Waters Treaty*

The main features of the Indus Waters Treaty include (i) the allocation of three Eastern Rivers of the system (Ravi, Sutlej and Beas) to India; (ii) the allocation

---

Consequently, the World Bank offered its good offices for discussing the dispute, and negotiating a settlement, and proposed that a solution to the problem be looked for based purely on technical and engineering grounds. On 18 November 1951, the President of the World Bank proposed the establishment of a working group of engineers for that purpose, which was accepted by both parties. Hence, and hitherto, the World Bank got fully involved and entangled in the Indus Basin and its intricacies. *See* Salman & Uprety, *Conflict and Cooperation*, supra note 30, at 44–61.

33 *The Indus Waters Treaty*, India-Pakistan, 19 September 1960, 419 U.N.T.S. 126. The Agreement was signed by Mr. Jawaharlal Nehru, Prime Minister of India, and Field Marshal Mohammad Ayub Khan, President of Pakistan. Mr. W. A. B. Iliff signed on behalf of the World Bank for certain articles and annexures specified in the Treaty; *see* infra note 34.

34 The World Bank signed the Treaty for certain purposes specified in the Treaty, namely, Articles V and X, and Annexures F, G and H. Article V 'Financial Provisions" deals with India's contribution to Pakistan of Pounds Sterling 62,060,000 for partial funding of the replacement works that Pakistan would construct as a result of allocation of the Eastern Rivers to India, and the termination of Pakistan's water rights on those rivers. The Indian contribution was made to the World Bank in ten equal annual installments, and credited to the Indus Basin Development Fund. Article V also deals with the Bank's responsibilities to manage the Indus Basin Development Fund. The Fund consisted of close to 800 million dollars grant funding from a number of donors, World Bank loans, in addition to the Indian contribution, with a total of US$1.3 billion. The Fund was used to finance the replacement works that Pakistan needed to end its reliance on the Eastern Rivers and to augment the flow of the Western Rivers. Such works included, *inter alia*, eight linked canals nearly 400 miles long for transferring water from the Western Rivers to areas formerly irrigated from the Eastern Rivers; two storage dams, the Tarbela on the Indus and the Mangla on the Jhelum; power stations; 2,500 tubewells; and other works to integrate the whole river and canal system within Pakistan. Article X deals with the 'Emergency Provision' and sets forth certain responsibilities for the Bank in case Pakistan was unable to obtain the necessary materials and equipment from abroad prior to 31 March 1965, because of the outbreak of large-scale international hostilities. Annexure H deals with 'Transitional Arrangements' to be undertaken during the transition period that started in 1960, and ended in 1970, in the course of which Pakistan was to construct the replacement works and end its reliance on the Eastern Rivers. The Bank's role and responsibilities under Articles V and X, and Annexure H were fully completed some time ago. Annexures F and G deal with 'Neutral Expert" and 'Court of Arbitration', respectively, in connection with settlement of differences and disputes, where the Bank has, and will continue to have, a limited procedural role. *See* S. M. A. Salman, '*The Baglihar Difference and its Resolution Process: A Triumph for the Indus Waters Treaty?*', 10 Water Policy (2008) 105–117.

of three Western Rivers (Indus, Jhelum and Chenab) to Pakistan; (iii) construction of replacement works by Pakistan to meet its Eastern Rivers needs from the Western Rivers; (iv) incorporation of safeguards in the Treaty to ensure unrestricted flow of waters in the Western Rivers, subject to some uses by India; (v) regular exchange of flow-data of rivers, canals, and streams between the parties; and (vi) constitution of a Permanent Indus Commission to oversee implementation of the Treaty.

It is worth mentioning that both nations rebuffed the idea of administering the Indus Basin as a single unit (an original idea proposed by the World Bank). The two parties and the World Bank had also discussed the idea of dividing the waters of the Indus River system between the two countries, which was eventually also discarded.[35] Unlike treaties in other basins that divide rivers by flow or quantity, the Indus Treaty divides the Indus system into three Eastern Rivers, to which India has 'unrestricted use', and three Western Rivers, to which Pakistan has 'unrestricted use' with, however, certain exceptions.

Pakistan agreed not to interfere with the waters of the Eastern Rivers where they formed boundaries between the two countries, and India retained the right to build upstream non-storage dams on the Western Rivers.[36] It was agreed that Pakistan would carry out infrastructure works during a 'transition period' to replace the canals on which it had relied for drawing water from the Eastern Rivers. During this transition period, India agreed to supply Pakistan with a minimum amount of water until Pakistan had completed its replacements works.[37] To help defray the costs of building this infrastructure, India agreed to pay a fixed sum of money to Pakistan (£62,060,000) and a consortium of donors provided Pakistan additional funds (US$800 million). The donors and the Indian contribution, together with the World Bank funding, totaling about US$1.3 billion, enabled Pakistan to build the Tarbela Dam on the Indus River and the Mangla Dam on the Jhelum River, creating sufficient storage to replace two-thirds of the water lost as a result of India's control of the three Eastern Rivers.[38]

35 *See* Salman & Uprety, *Conflict and Cooperation*, supra note 30, at 46.

36 *See* Indus Waters Treaty, supra note 33, Article II (2), which includes the exceptions on the Eastern Rivers, and Article III (2), which contains the exceptions on the Western Rivers.

37 Under Article II (2)(9) of the Treaty, the Transition Period is defined as extending from 1960 until 1970, with a possible three-year extension. Article IV (1) of the Treaty included detailed provisions on Pakistan's rights and obligations during the Transition Period.

38 *See* C. M. Ali, *The Emergence of Pakistan* (New York: Columbia University Press, 1967) at 330; *see also* generally, N. D. Gulhati, *Indus Waters Treaty: An Exercise in International Mediation* (New Delhi: Allied Publishers, 1973).

A noteworthy legal point, as per a provision of the Treaty, is that nothing contained in the Treaty is to be construed as constituting a recognition or waiver of any rights or claims whatsoever other than those expressly recognized or waived, and most importantly, as in any way establishing any general principle of law or any precedent.[39] This language has raised concerns amongst *opinio juris* regarding its effect and interpretation in the future.[40]

The articles of the Treaty range from provisions on the division of the rivers, financial issues, the exchange of data, and cooperation in the future. From the preamble, the emphasis is put on the interdependent relationship of the two countries on the Indus River system. The Treaty not only states the rights and obligations of one to the other concerning the use of the waters, but also the importance of communication and exchange of data and information. The first article clearly defines the tributaries of the Indus River system, and distinguishes between the Eastern and the Western Rivers, and describes the three main uses that come forward in the Treaty, namely, (1) agricultural use, (2) domestic use, and (3) non-consumptive use.[41]

To further and facilitate communication between the two parties, the Treaty provides for 'exchange of data.' It specifies the range of data that should be transmitted monthly to one another by each party. They include (a) daily (or as observed or estimated less frequently) gauge and discharge data relating to flow of the rivers at all observation sites; (b) daily extractions for or releases from reservoirs; (c) daily withdrawals at the heads of all canals operated by governments, including link canals; (d) daily escapages from all canals, including link canals; and (e) daily deliveries from link canals. The Treaty further

39 Indus Waters Treaty, supra note 33, art. XI (2).

40 Due to this provision, Professor McCaffrey believes that the two countries could presumably revert to their fundamental legal postures in any future water disputes that was not governed by the Indus Treaty. *See* S. C. McCaffrey, '*Water, Politics and International Law*', in P. H. Gleick (ed.), *Water in Crisis: A Guide to the World's Fresh Water Resources* (New York: Oxford University Press, 1993) 92–104, at 95. However, Professor Baxter considers that despite the stated intention of the Treaty, a provision of this nature cannot keep others from looking to the settlement as a precedent or from deriving whatever general principles they choose from the terms agreed upon. *See* R. R. Baxter, '*The Indus Basin*', in A. H. Garretson et al. (eds.), *The Law of International Drainage Basins* (Dobbs Ferry, NY: Oceana Publications, 1967) 449–457, at 456. Along those lines, Professor Lipper, citing this attempt 'expressly to negate any precedential value (the Treaty) might otherwise have,' commented that 'if the general thesis were to be accepted that treaties were mere bargains without international law-making effect, a major source of international law would be eliminated. Fortunately, no such thesis has found its way into international legal practice.' *See* J. Lipper, '*Equitable Utilization*', in Garreston et al., *id.*, 15–88, at 35. The authors of this monograph subscribe fully to this latter view and conclusion.

41 Indus Waters Treaty, supra note 33, definitions (9), (10) and (11) respectively, art. I.

states that other available data related to any provision of the Treaty should be supplied to the other party, and vice versa, on request.[42]

The two parties' common interests are emphasized and confirmed throughout the Treaty. The parties recognize that they have a common interest in the optimum development of the rivers, and, to that end, declare their intention to cooperate, by agreement, to the fullest possible extent.[43] The Treaty also includes provisions in relation to the future on sharing information about possible plans or engineering projects on the rivers.[44] Most importantly it includes detailed provisions on notification, and states:

> If either Party plans to construct any engineering work which would cause interference with the waters of any of the rivers and which in its opinion, would affect the other Party materially, it shall notify the other Party of its plans and shall supply such data relating to the work as may be available and as would enable the other Party to inform itself of the nature, magnitude and effect of the work. If a work would cause interference with the waters of any of the rivers but would not, in the opinion of the Party planning it, affect the other party materially, nevertheless the Party planning the work shall, on request, supply the other party with such data regarding the nature, magnitude and effect, if any, of the work as may be available.[45]

2.1.1.3 *Governance and Dispute Resolution*

The institutional arrangements that form part of the Treaty are elaborated in Article VIII. For purposes of monitoring implementation, the Indus Waters Treaty established a two-member Permanent Indus Commission (PIC), with a commissioner each from India and Pakistan,[46] granting it a role, among others, in the initial resolution of disputes. Each Commissioner is a representative of his government for all matters arising out of the Treaty and serves as the regular channel of communication on matters relating to the implementation of the Treaty.

The main purpose of the PIC is thus to establish and maintain cooperative arrangements for the implementation of the Treaty, to promote cooperation between the two parties in development of the waters of the rivers of the Indus

---

42 *Id.*, art. VI (2).
43 *Id.*, preamble and art VII.
44 *Id.*, art. VII.
45 *Id.*, art. VII (2).
46 *Id.*, art. VIII.

system, and to settle promptly any questions arising between the parties and to identify any possible problem that could arise.[47] While the PIC is also required to undertake periodical inspection of the Indus system to determine the facts concerning development and work on the rivers,[48] the Commissioners are obligated to meet at least once a year, alternately in India and Pakistan, and to report to each government annually and whenever considered necessary.[49]

Elaborate provisions concerning the settlement of differences and disputes are included in Article IX, and Annexures F and G of the Treaty. Article IX states that any question that arises between the two parties concerning the interpretation or application of the Treaty, or the existence of any fact which, if established, might constitute a breach of this Treaty, shall first be examined by the Permanent Indus Commission (PIC), which will endeavor to resolve the question by agreement. If the PIC does not reach agreement on such a question, then the question is elevated, and a difference will be deemed to have arisen.

Such an elevated question shall be dealt with in either of two ways. First, any difference that in the opinion of either Commissioner falls within the ambit of the 23 questions enumerated in Part 1 of Annexure F shall, at the request of either Commissioner, be dealt with by a Neutral Expert in accordance with the provisions of Annexure F of the Treaty.[50] Second, if the difference does not come within the 23 questions enumerated in Paragraph 1 of Annexure F, or if a Neutral Expert has informed the Commission that, in his opinion, the difference, or part thereof, should be treated as a dispute, then a dispute will be deemed to have arisen.[51] Such a dispute will be resolved through a court of arbitration in accordance with the provisions of Annexure G of the Treaty. Furthermore, the PIC also has the discretion of dealing with the elevated question either as a difference to be referred to the Neutral Expert, or as a dispute to be resolved through a court of arbitration.[52]

If the other party agrees with the determination of the aggrieved party that the question be dealt with as a difference, then the two parties will endeavor to appoint the Neutral Expert themselves.[53] If they fail to agree on a Neutral Expert, then they will try to agree on a third party who would undertake the task of such an appointment. If that attempt also fails, then the World Bank is

47 *Id.*, art. VIII (4).
48 *Id.*, art. VIII (4)(c) and (d).
49 *Id.*, art. VIII (5).
50 *Id.*, art. IX (2)(a).
51 *Id.*, art. IX (2)(b).
52 *Id.*, art. IX (2)(b) (Proviso).
53 *Id.*, art. IX (3).

required under the Treaty, at the request of the aggrieved party, to appoint the Neutral Expert, who should be a highly qualified engineer.[54] How the matter is to be laid before the Neutral Expert, and how it is to be resolved by him/her, are the subjects of detailed provisions in Annexure F of the Treaty.[55] It should be emphasized, however, that the Neutral Expert's determination on all matters within his/her competence is final and binding, and is not appealable to the court of arbitration.[56]

A court of arbitration shall be established to resolve a dispute in accordance with the provisions of Annexure G under one of three circumstances. The first is upon agreement between the two parties to do so, as discussed above. The second is at the request of either party, if, after negotiations, the opinion of the aggrieved party is that the dispute is not likely to be resolved by negotiation or mediation. Third, if the difference does not come within the ambit of the 23 questions enumerated in Annexure F, or if the Neutral Expert decides that the difference or any part thereof should be treated as a dispute, then the PIC shall send a report to this effect to the two governments.[57] If the aggrieved party, one month after receipt of the report, comes to the conclusion that the other party 'is unduly delaying the negotiations', then that party may request the establishment of a court of arbitration.[58]

A court of arbitration is to consist of seven members, two to be designated by each of the two parties, and the other three (called umpires) to be selected by agreement of the parties or, by one or more persons agreed upon by the two parties.[59] Failing that, the selection of the three umpires shall be through a lengthy process which involves the Secretary-General of the United Nations or the President of the World Bank; the President of the Massachusetts Institute of Technology in the United States, or the Rector of the Imperial College of Science and Technology, London; and the Chief Justice of the United States or the Lord Chief Justice of England.[60]

The three neutral umpires are to be, respectively, a person qualified to be chairman of the court of arbitration, an engineer, and an international lawyer. Quite interestingly, the court of arbitration does not consist entirely

54 *See id.*, Annexure F, para. 4(a). The World Bank was also shouldered with the responsibility of appointing the Neutral Expert during the transition period.

55 *Id.*, Annexure F.

56 *Id.*, Annexure F, para. 11.

57 *Id.*, art. IX (2)(b) and Annexure F, para. 7.

58 For detail, *see* Salman & Uprety, *Conflict and Cooperation*, supra note 30, at 53.

59 Indus Waters Treaty, supra note 33, Annexure G, para. 4.

60 For details of the process of the court of arbitration *see id.*, art. IX and Annexure G.

of lawyers.[61] The parties are to endeavor to put together a Standing Panel of Umpires from whom the selection might be made. It is noteworthy that the applicable law includes the Treaty and, for purposes of the interpretation and application of the Treaty in priority, (i) the international conventions establishing the rules explicitly recognized by India and Pakistan and (ii) customary international law.[62]

What issue should be labelled as a dispute is not explicitly stated in the Treaty. However, the Treaty explains what can be considered interference with the waters, and also states that insignificant interference can be ignored.[63] Defining interference in such a vague manner leaves a lot of room for differences.[64]

It is worth noting that the process for settlement of differences and disputes under the Treaty is not hierarchical. A question is referred to the Neutral Expert not as an appeal of the decision of the Commission. Rather, it is referred to the Neutral Expert because the Commission was not able to resolve it, or it falls within some specified issues under the Treaty. Failure to resolve contentious or difficult questions should be expected given that the Commission consists of two persons, each representing one of the two countries. Moreover, as noted above, the decision of the Neutral Expert is final and binding, and the Treaty emphasizes that such a decision is binding not just on the parties, but also on any court of arbitration to be established.[65]

Thus, the more than 150-page long treaty, the outcome of close to 10 years long negotiations by India and Pakistan, under the good offices/mediation of the World Bank, addressed most issues surrounding the Indus Basin. It has not only provided for the Basin's division, but also adequately covered the consequences of such division, including dispute settlement, in a very comprehensive manner.

2.1.1.4 *Role of the World Bank in the Indus Waters Treaty Negotiations and Conclusion*

Several strategic, tactical as well as logistical actions by the Bank contributed to the success of the Indus Treaty negotiations. First and foremost was the Bank's

---

61 Per this provision and the stipulation that the Neutral Expert should be a highly qualified engineer, the Indus Waters Treaty gives a clear role and prominence to engineers in resolution of contested issues. It should be added that the Permanent Indus Commission, which is authorized to adjudicate questions, usually consists of two engineers.

62 For detail, *see* Salman & Uprety, *Conflict and Cooperation*, supra note 30, at 54.

63 Indus Waters Treaty, supra note 33, art. I (15).

64 *Id.* (proviso).

65 *See id.*, Annexure F, para. 11.

continued active involvement at the highest level. From the very start, Eugene Black, the then President of the World Bank, was personally and directly involved in the attempts to resolve the dispute. The offer of the good offices of the Bank was sent by him to the prime ministers of India and Pakistan,[66] with whom he corresponded regularly, offering ideas and urging concessions. He visited India and Pakistan in February 1952 where he met with both prime ministers, thus establishing a personal relationship with each of them. As a result, an agreement was reached in March 1952 outlining an approach for developing joint planning for the Indus Basin Irrigation System.

The Bank appointed Mr. Raymond Wheeler, an engineering adviser, in May 1952, to work with the two teams of engineers. Mr. Wheeler continued working with the two teams, and after the joint planning approach was abandoned in September 1953, Mr. Wheeler was replaced in 1954 by Mr. William Iliff, assistant to the President at the time, as the Bank's chief mediator.[67] Mr. Iliff was appointed as Vice President later, but he continued to lead the Bank's team. Mr. Black continued to be engaged, and visited India and Pakistan again in 1958, as well as in 1959, to work out the details of the agreement.[68] The World Bank was so proactive that some scholars termed the intervention as 'continuing conciliation.'[69] This active and continued involvement by the Bank at the highest level must have sent a clear signal to the parties regarding the

66 *See* E. S. Mason & R. E. Asher, *The World Bank Since Bretton Woods* (Washington, DC: Brookings Institution, 1973) at 612. Both prime ministers replied on 25 September 1951, accepting the Bank's offer.

67 Mr. Black wrote to the parties on 13 August 1954 that 'The Bank group taking part in these discussions will be under the direct guidance of the Bank's management. Mr. Garner and I intend to keep closely in touch with all phases of the work and to be available for participation when necessary. However, I think, that the management will have to play not only a more active, but also a more continuous, role than it did in the earlier phase of the Bank's participation, and we have therefore decided that Mr. Iliff will represent management as day-to-day head of the Bank team….' For the content of the letter, *see* Gulhati, supra note 38, at 170–172. Mr. Robert L. Garner was Vice President of the Bank at that time.

68 Information collected by the authors from the World Bank archives. In their 1959 visit, Black and Iliff carried with them the final heads of agreement of an Indus Waters Treaty which were discussed with the prime ministers of India and Pakistan.

69 *See* Baxter, supra note 40, at 477 (stating that the Bank pursued its own inquiries into the facts, and suggested at various stages, principles upon which agreements may be based, calling this process 'continuing conciliation'). As stated above, the Bank offered to both parties in 1951 its 'good offices'. The Bank's intervention in the Indus dispute is usually referred to as 'mediation'. This variation in the terms given to the Bank intervention underscores the difficulties in classifying the intervention, particularly at the beginning and during the process, and explains why the term mediation is used in a generic sense to refer to any of the three modes of intervention.

determination of the World Bank to reach a fair and acceptable resolution to the dispute.

Equally important was the fact that the Bank did not come with a fixed, rigid blueprint for the resolution of the dispute. Its initial approach, as alluded to above, was to develop joint planning for the Indus irrigation system, as recommended by Mr. Lilienthal. However, when it became clear to the Bank that this approach was not acceptable to the parties, the Bank abandoned that approach. It asked the parties in September 1953 to prepare their own individual plans. Those plans, which were based on the idea of separate, as opposed to joint, development of the Indus Basin, were presented in October 1953.[70] Based on those plans, the Bank developed in 1954 its own proposal which called for the allocation of the Eastern rivers exclusively to India and the Western rivers exclusively to Pakistan.[71] However, when Pakistan objected to this proposal claiming that there were not enough waters in the Western Rivers to replace Pakistan's existing uses of the Eastern Rivers, the Bank agreed to revisit the matter. After further studies, it agreed with Pakistan and issued an aide memoire on 21 May 1956, adjusting its 1954 proposal, by including the need for additional storage reservoirs in the Western Rivers to provide Pakistan with an adequate supply of water.[72]

Another reason for the Bank's success was its ability to obtain concessions from both parties throughout the duration of its mediation. The first concession was that neither party would take any action to reduce the flow of waters to the other. When Pakistan decided to walk out of the negotiations to show their disagreement with the Bank's proposal of allocating the rivers of the

---

70 The Indian plan allocated 29 million acre-feet (MAF) of the waters of the Indus to India and 90 MAF to Pakistan (the total being 119 MAF). The Pakistani plan allocated 15.5 MAF to India and 102.5 MAF to Pakistan (the total being 118 MAF). After discussion and negotiations, the Indian plan was further developed by allocating all the Eastern Rivers (the Sutlej, the Ravi and the Beas) and 7% of the Western Rivers (the Indus, the Jhelum and the Chenab) to India and none of the Eastern Rivers and 93% of the Western Rivers to Pakistan. On the other hand, the revised Pakistani plan allocated 30% of the Eastern Rivers and none of the Western Rivers to India and 70% of the Eastern Rivers and all the Western Rivers to Pakistan. For discussion of those plans *see* Gulhati, supra note 38, Chapters VI and VII. *See also*, generally, J. Vivekanandan & S. Nair, '*Climate Change and Water: Examining the Interlinkages*', in D. Michel & A. Pandya (eds.), *Troubled Waters: Climate Change, Hydropolitics, and Transboundary Resources* (Washington, DC: The Henry L. Stimson Center, 2009), at 1–14, and A. K. Biswas, '*Indus Waters Treaty: The Negotiating Process*', 17:4 Water International (1992) 201–209.

71 The Bank's plan further envisaged a transition period of five years during which India would continue supplying Pakistan with waters from the Eastern Rivers, while Pakistan would construct the necessary works for tapping alternative sources of waters.

72 *See* Baxter, supra note 40, at 460–465.

Indus system, the Bank threatened that if negotiations were not resumed, the Bank would end its mediation, and make the reasons known publicly, thus extending its persuasion to pressure.[73] This prompted Pakistan to reconsider its decision. When India decided that the negotiations were dragging on for too long, and that India was no longer bound by the 1952 Standstill Agreement, the Bank intervened and persuaded India to stick to the Agreement. Furthermore, Pakistan was persuaded to abandon its claims to waters from the Eastern Rivers and India to contribute to Pakistan's replacement work.[74]

The development plans of the two countries depended at that time, to a large extent, upon loans from the Bank, and that gave the Bank more leverage and influence. As a matter of fact, the Bank's own lending, as well as its borrowing programs, were affected by the Indus dispute, which provided another reason for its pro-active involvement. Equally important, because of the dispute, the Bank was unable to finance the Bhakra-Nangal project in India, or the Lower Sind Barrage project in Pakistan.[75] As President Eugene Black stated:

> Not only did the Indus issue stand in the way of constructive action by the Bank in the subcontinent, it was cause for concern in a wider sense. With two of the Bank's potentially largest customers so bitterly opposed, the world's investors might regard the Bank's own prospects with a skepticism that would cripple its ability to raise money through borrowing.[76]

After adjusting its proposal regarding allocation of the rivers to take into account Pakistan's concerns, the Bank realized the need for additional financing for the huge cost of the works that were required to implement the agreement.[77] Without the funds for carrying out such works, there would simply be no agreement. The Bank was, however, successful in mobilizing those funds and largely on a grant basis, and created the Indus Basin Development

73 *See* Mason & Asher, supra note 66, at 617.

74 *See* generally Salman & Uprety, *Conflict and Cooperation*, supra note 30, at 53.

75 *See* S. M. A. Salman, *The World Bank Policy for Projects on International Waterways: An Historical and Legal Analysis* (Leiden: Martinus Nijhoff Publishers, 2009; Washington, DC: The World Bank, 2009) at 23–24.

76 *See* Mason & Asher, supra note 66, at 612, quoting Eugene R. Black, '*The Indus: A Moral for Nations*', New York Times (11 December 1960).

77 The World Bank made a distinction between works needed to replace water when the Basin was divided between India and Pakistan (replacement works) and the development works desired to enhance water use by both countries. It was agreed only development works would be financed under the Fund. *See* generally, S. S. Kirmani, '*Water, Peace and Conflict Management: The Experience of the Indus and Mekong River Basins*', 15:4 Water International (1990) 200–205, at 201–202.

Fund (which consisted, as mentioned above, of a total of US$1.3 billion). The ability to raise all those funds, no doubt, gave the Bank tremendous strength in successfully concluding the mediation process.

As alluded to above, the Bank was willing to accept a wide range of responsibilities in the implementation of the arrangements under the Treaty. Accordingly, the Bank became a signatory to the Indus Waters Treaty for the purposes specified in Articles V and X, and Annexures F, G, and H.[78]

Another important factor for the success of the Bank mediation effort was its ability to delink the Indus dispute from other disputes between the two countries (particularly the Kashmir territorial dispute). Indeed, India and Pakistan continued to honor their commitments under the Indus Waters Treaty even during the times of tensions over other disputes, particularly over Kashmir.[79] The Treaty survived the 1965 and the 1971 India-Pakistan wars, as well as the acute tension on the sub-continent in 2002. This situation stands out in sharp contrast to the situation between India and China where the borders disputes have often derailed discussions, and even negatively affected some existing arrangements, on the shared water resources between the two states.[80]

The Bank's role, no doubt, was crucial in the resolution of the Indus Waters dispute, and the finalization of the Treaty and its early implementation.[81] The Herculean effort by the Bank in bringing India and Pakistan to the negotiating table and keeping them there for close to 10 years until the Treaty was signed is a testimony to the Bank's commitment to resolving the dispute.[82] As such, its role has been summed up by some experts as proactive, neutral, pragmatic, and fair.[83]

---

78 *See* supra note 34 and accompanying text.

79 It should be noted in this context that India continued to make installment payments for its share of the cost of the replacement works to the Indus Basin Fund administered by the World Bank even during times of war between India and Pakistan. Similarly, the Permanent Indus Commission continued to hold its annual meeting even during the periods of heightened tension between the two countries.

80 *See* infra note 256 (Time magazine report).

81 For additional information on the role of the World Bank in the Indus Waters Treaty, *see* 'Foreword' by Sir William Iliff, in Gulhati, supra note 38. *See also* Mason & Asher, supra note 66, at 610–627; Salman & Uprety, *Conflict and Cooperation,* supra note 30, at 44–61.

82 For a comparison of the role of the Bank on the Indus dispute with the American role on the Jordan River and with the role of the Bank itself on the Nile Basin, *see* Salman, '*Mediation of International Water Disputes—The Indus, the Jordan and the Nile Basins Interventions*', in L. Boisson de Chazournes et al. (eds.), *International Law and Freshwater: The Multiple Challenges* (Cheltenham: Edward Elgar, 2013) at 360–405.

83 *See* S. Kirmani and G. Le Moigne, 'Fostering Riparian Cooperation in International River Basins, The World Bank at its Best in Development Diplomacy', Technical Paper No. 335, *World Bank* (Washington, DC, 1997) at 5.

2.1.1.5 *Unique Features of the Indus Waters Treaty*

The Indus Waters Treaty displays a few features that are quite unique and distinguish it from other international water treaties. The first unique feature is the division of the six rivers of the Indus system, rather than the waters of these rivers, between the two parties. This solution was arrived at after the failure of the parties to divide the waters of the rivers. It was resorted to after lengthy soul searching and conviction, including by the mediator, the World Bank.

A second unique feature is that the Indus Waters Treaty is the only international water treaty to be signed by a third party for certain specified purposes.[84] As discussed in the previous section of this monograph, this third party, the World Bank, played a considerable role in mediation by using its convening power and the leverage of its cross-sector financing. It still retains a major role in the resolution of differences and disputes arising under the Treaty between India and Pakistan.

Moreover, in connection with the World Bank's role in the appointment of a Neutral Expert for resolution of differences arising between the two parties, the Treaty set up the first ever trust fund to be administered by the World Bank. The purpose of the trust fund is the financing of the cost of the Neutral Expert.[85] As will be discussed below, this trust fund was used 45 years after its establishment to finance the Neutral Expert in the context of the Baglihar difference.

A third unique feature of the Treaty is that it entered into force and was in effect retroactively. This is very unusual because, generally, treaties are signed, and then ratified, and they enter into force either on the day of ratification, or on a specified date falling thereafter. The Indus Waters Treaty was signed on September 19, 1960 and the instruments of ratification were exchanged on 12 January 1961. Yet, Article XII (2) of the Treaty stipulated that entry into force of the Treaty would take effect retrospectively from the first of April 1960, five months before the Treaty itself was signed. The reason for this unusual arrangement related to agreements signed by India and Pakistan, starting in

---

84 The purposes for which the World Bank signed the Indus Waters Treaty are discussed in supra note 34.

85 Annexure F lays down detailed provisions on the cost of the process of the Neutral Expert. The Treaty established a trust fund with the World Bank where each of the two parties was required to deposit US$5,000. This turned to be the first trust fund ever established and administered by the World Bank. The trust fund would initially cover the cost of the Neutral Expert, and each party was required to initially meet its own cost. However, the Neutral Expert has the authority of determining, as part of the award, which of the two parties should bear the entire cost of the process. More details will be discussed below in this Part.

1948, under which India was to supply Pakistan with water from the Central Bari Doab Canal of the Ravi River until 31 March 1960.[86] Accordingly, it was agreed during negotiations of the Treaty that the Transition Period would start on 1 April 1960. It was therefore necessary for the Treaty to become effective as of that date.[87]

Another unique feature of the Treaty is the varying process, mechanisms, and institutions for the settlement of issues that may arise between India and Pakistan, and the gradual elevation of the process from question, to difference, and then to dispute, without a hierarchical character. This monograph will discuss such features below.

2.1.1.6 *Dispute Resolution Mechanisms Tested*

The Indus Waters Treaty set in motion complex and intricate dispute settlement procedures and mechanisms. This complex process started to unfold some 20 years after the Treaty was concluded, and the mechanisms were invoked in a few cases.

2.1.1.6.1 The 'Tulbul' or 'Wullar' Barrage Question

The first time India and Pakistan invoked the dispute resolution process under the Indus Waters Treaty was in relation to the Wullar Barrage. It started with a disagreement pertaining to the construction of a barrage by India under the Tulbul Navigation Project (referred to by Pakistan as the Wullar Barrage), where the Jhelum River flows into Lake Wullar from the south and flows out of it from the west. India began construction of the barrage on the Jhelum River in 1984 to augment water supplies in Wullar Lake in Indian held Kashmir,[88] to be used in the lean period, and to improve navigability of the river between the cities of Srinagar and Baramullah.[89]

Allegedly affected, Pakistan referred the issue to the Permanent Indus Commission (PIC) in 1986, but the PIC failed to resolve it. Pakistan then decided to refer the issue to a court of arbitration, at which point India suspended construction work. In 1989, Pakistan agreed to the construction of the Barrage conditional to Pakistani inspection, which India rejected. The two sides

---

86 *See* supra note 30.

87 *See* Indus Waters Treaty, supra note 33, art. XII (2).

88 *See* E. Condon et al., *Resource Disputes in South Asia: Water Scarcity and the Potential for Interstate Conflict*, Report Prepared for the Office of South Asia Analysis, U.S. Central Intelligence Agency, Workshop in International Public Affairs, 1 June 2009 (University of Madison, Wisconsin, 2009) at 7.

89 A. Yaqoob, *International River Waters in South Asia: Source of Conflict or Cooperation?* (Islamabad: Pakistan Institute of Regional Studies, date unknown) at 134.

had almost reached an agreement in October 1991, whereby India would keep 6.2 meters of the Barrage ungated with a crest length of 1,574.9 meters, and would forgo the storage capacity of 370,044,551 m^3 allowing, in return, the water level in the Barrage to attain the full operational level of 1,578.22 meters. However, in February 1992, Pakistan introduced another condition when it asked India to drop the idea of implementing a project on the Neelum River (the Kishenganga Hydroelectric Project),[90] which would affect Pakistan's Neelum-Jhelum Power-generation Project (in Punjab). The condition was unacceptable to India.

It must be recalled that the Jhelum River is one of the Western Rivers, over whose waters Pakistan has exclusive rights. India is not permitted under the Indus Waters Treaty to build storage facilities upstream on those rivers except in limited amounts for purposes of flood control.

Pakistan protested the construction on the Jhelum River on three grounds.[91] First, it argued that India was violating the Indus Waters Treaty by constructing a storage facility upstream. Second, Pakistan claimed the barrage would change the volume of daily water flow. Third, it alleged the barrage would harm Pakistan's canal system downstream. In response, India maintained that the project was not meant for storage but for flood control purposes, which are permitted under the Treaty, and that the project would regulate the flow of the River, ultimately resulting in benefits for both states.[92] Amidst Pakistani objections, India temporarily halted the construction work in 1987 despite its counterarguments. To date, the construction remains suspended, and there have been a few rounds of talks, but the issue remains unresolved. India, maintaining the idea of the project, has tried to renegotiate the matter. The two countries met at the Secretary level in May 2011 in Islamabad,[93] and in March 2012 in New Delhi,[94] but were not able to make any progress in resolving the issue. However, both sides have emphasized the need for an early and amicable resolution of the issue within the ambit of the Indus Waters Treaty.[95]

The Tulbul Navigation/Wullar Barrage Project remains on the political agenda of the two states and has contributed to tensions between them. India's

---

90 *See* infra note 122 and accompanying text.

91 *See* Condon et al. supra note 88, at 7.

92 I. M. Sahai, *'Baglihar Decision—An End to the Dispute?'*, 59:4 International Water Power and Dam Construction (2007) at 14–16.

93 R. Tiwari, *'Tulbul Project: India-Pak Talks Today'*, The Indian Express (11 May 2011), http://archive.indianexpress.com/news/tulbul-project-indiapak-talks-today/788727/.

94 Government of India, Ministry of External Affairs, *India-Pakistan Joint Statement on Tulbul Navigation/Wullar Barrage Project*, 28 March 2012.

95 *Id.*

interference in the Western Rivers over which Pakistan has exclusive rights continues to provoke the latter, fueled by the distrust that exists between the two neighbors. Even though both parties emphasize the need for an amicable solution, not much has been done to build the trust with the aim of reaching a solution. With mutual distrust and constant suspicions, it would seem difficult for the two states to reach an agreement and resolve the issue, which does not appear to be very complex. The situation, however, has also opened the door for more issues to arise between the parties as well as a search for other mechanisms, as provided by the Treaty, to resolve them.

2.1.1.6.2 The Baglihar Difference

Another controversy arose around 1999 involving a hydropower project (Baglihar Dam Project). India planned to construct a dam, sixty miles upstream from the Pakistani border, on the Chenab River, one of the Western Rivers allocated under the Treaty to Pakistan (subject to India's right to build upstream non-storage facilities). India claimed its right to build upstream non-storage facilities on the Chenab under the Indus Treaty.

Consisting of a 429-foot high and 1,046-foot long dam across the Chenab River, which would have a storage capacity of 321,000 acre-feet (395,947,672 m^3), this 900-megawatt hydro-electricity generation project was planned in two phases. The first phase of the project was completed in 2004 and the second phase in 2008.[96]

Pakistan was concerned that the planned submerged gated spillways of the Baglihar Dam might allow India to manipulate the storage of water to Pakistan's disadvantage. Pakistan was of the view that the design of the Dam violated the Treaty, as it would affect the flow of the Chenab River, which would ultimately cause water shortages in Pakistan.[97]

As the matter could not be resolved amicably, Pakistan invoked the Indus Waters Treaty's dispute resolution mechanism, as it believed the proposed water storing capacity of the Baglihar Dam was at a level prohibited under the Treaty and the design of the hydropower plant violated several conditions spelled out therein. Pakistan was further concerned that the Baglihar Dam would allow India to obstruct and control the flow of the Chenab River. India, on the other hand, disagreeing with the claims of Pakistan, stated that the Baglihar Dam was merely planned as a run-of-river generation power plant

96 *See 'Baglihar Dam'*, https://wiki2.org/en/Baglihar_Dam (visited 3 March 2018).

97 *See* S. M. Tariq, *Pakistan-India Relations: Implementation of Indus Waters Treaty: A Pakistani Narrative*, background paper published by Pakistan Institute of Legislative Development and Transparency, Islamabad (December 2010) at 12.

without storage, and thus the design of the Dam did not violate the Indus Waters Treaty, and indeed, it was within its prescribed parameters.[98]

It should be noted that Pakistan had formally objected to the design of the Dam in 1999,[99] and talks between the two countries began in 2000 to try to resolve the question.[100] However, the process was complicated by the fact that Pakistani engineers could only visit the site in October 2003, after much reluctance from India. As expected, the talks did not yield any results and the impasse remained, contributing to the increase of tension between the two countries.

2.1.1.6.2.1 *Role for the Neutral Expert*

Following the failure to resolve the question through the Permanent Indus Commission, Pakistan, on 15 January 2005, approached the World Bank requesting that it appoint, as per the Indus Waters Treaty, a Neutral Expert to resolve the differences over the Baglihar Dam. In keeping with Article IX and Annexure F of the Treaty, and after a complex process involving a series of communications and consultations with the two parties, the Neutral Expert, Professor Raymond Lafitte of the Federal Institute of Technology at Lausanne, Switzerland, was appointed on 25 April 2005, more than three months after the request of Pakistan was submitted to the World Bank.[101]

---

98 *See* generally, Salman, *The Baglihar Difference*, supra note 34.

99 Yaqoob, supra note 89, at 136.

100 Condon et al., supra note 88, at 6.

101 The road the Bank had to take from the day it received the request of Pakistan (15 January 2005) to the day of the appointment of the Neutral Expert (25 April 2005) was turbulent and complex, and included, *inter alia*, the following:

First: The series of communications between the World Bank and the two parties included the request by Pakistan to the Bank to appoint the Neutral Expert; the reply of India to that request (where India claimed that the issue was still a question before the PIC, and the Bank should not interfere); the response of Pakistan to that reply; and a final reply from India. Each party got two rounds to make its claims or counterclaims. Pakistan demanded a third round, alleging that the first round was the initial submission of the claim, and that it should not count. However, the Bank rejected that argument.

Second: The Bank issued a memorandum to the two parties indicating that all communications with the Bank had to be in writing and that each document submitted to the Bank by one party would be shared with the other party. The Bank indicated further that all meetings would be trilateral, and no bilateral meetings on the Baglihar difference would take place.

Third: Pakistan asked the World Bank at the beginning of the process of appointing the Neutral Expert to issue a provisional order to India to halt construction of the Dam until the decision of the Neutral Expert was issued. The Bank declined, indicating that its role is confined solely to the appointment of the Neutral Expert.

The Bank handed over the process to Professor Lafitte on 9 June 2005, following his acceptance to act as the Neutral Expert. The handover took place during the first meeting, which was also attended by representatives of the two parties and was held at the World Bank Office in Paris. During that meeting the basic rules and procedures for the conduct of the process, as well as the work program, were discussed and agreed upon, keeping in mind the Treaty

Fourth: Following a thorough examination of the documents submitted by the two parties and the Treaty, the Bank lawyers concluded that the Bank was required under the Treaty to appoint a Neutral Expert. Nonetheless, Bank management decided to seek a second outside opinion on the matter from an ICJ judge. Interestingly, the ICJ judge confirmed the Bank lawyers' findings without any additions or changes.

Fifth: Subsequent to its decision that the Bank was required to appoint the Neutral Expert, the Bank had to determine what constitutes 'consultations' with the two parties prior to appointing the Neutral Expert, as required under the Treaty. The Bank decided, after an extensive search, to prepare a list of 20 eminent engineers from which to choose the Neutral Expert. Each engineer was interviewed at length to ensure that there were no issues of conflict of interest; seven were included in the final list of potential Neutral Experts after each confirmed their agreement to serve as the Neutral Expert, if selected.

Sixth: The plan was to submit three names to the two parties in the first round, and if the two parties did not agree on one candidate, then the Bank would submit the second list with three new candidates. If the parties failed again to agree on one candidate, then the Bank would appoint the seventh candidate. That process, for the Bank, would constitute 'consultations' as required under the Treaty. However, the two parties agreed on one candidate, Professor Raymond Lafitte, during the first round of consultations. That spared the Bank the two remaining rounds of consultations.

Seventh: Consequently, the Bank notified Professor Lafitte of his appointment as the Neutral Expert. Upon his acceptance, the Bank explained to him that the Bank role was completed with his appointment, and clarified that he would not be getting technical or legal advice from the World Bank. Mr. Lafitte sought the views of the World Bank on the appointment of an assistant and a legal adviser, and the Bank advised him that he should get the prior approval of the two parties for the person to be appointed as his legal adviser, which he did.

Eighth: It was agreed among the World Bank, the Neutral Expert, and India and Pakistan that the report of the Neutral Expert would be the property of India and Pakistan. However, the Bank, pointing at the extensive global interest in the Baglihar difference and the Neutral Expert process and the outcome, and the need for some transparency, proposed that an Executive Summary of the report of the Neutral Expert be prepared and disclosed to the public. This proposal was accepted by the parties and the Neutral Expert. Thus, the tasks that the Bank undertook from the day of the request to the appointment of the Neutral Expert, and which lasted for more than three months, showed clearly that the process of the appointment of the Neutral Expert had transformed itself from a simple administrative role as conceived under the Treaty, to a quasi-judicial task in actual practice. For a detailed summary and analysis of the Baglihar difference, the process for resolving it, and the outcome, *see* Salman, *The Baglihar Difference*, supra note 34.

requirement that the decision by the Neutral Expert should be rendered as soon as possible.[102]

A timetable was set (it was adjusted later), which would start with India providing by July 15, 2005, the information specified in Appendix II to Annexure D, referred to above. Pakistan would provide its memorial by August and India its counter-memorial by September 2005. Pakistan would file its reply by January 2006, and India its rejoinder by March 2006. The draft determination of the Neutral Expert would be completed by early October 2006, and the parties' written comments would be submitted by the end of October 2006. In November 2006 the parties would provide additional written comments. The final determination of the Neutral Expert would be rendered by February 2007. It was also agreed that four more meetings would be held before the Neutral Expert would finalize and issue his decision.[103]

The sequence of the written procedures was adopted from the practice of the International Centre for Settlement of Investment Disputes (ICSID), which provides for two possible rounds of exchange of documents between the parties as well as for following each written procedure with an oral one. It was further agreed by the four parties (India, Pakistan, the World Bank, and the Neutral Expert) that ICSID would act as the secretariat for the Neutral Expert process.[104]

Following submission by Pakistan and India of the basic information and memoranda agreed upon, the Neutral Expert shared a draft determination with the two parties, asking for their written and oral comments. Finally, in Switzerland, on 12 February 2007, the Neutral Expert delivered to the ambassadors of India and Pakistan, signed copies of the final decision on the Baglihar difference (referred to as the Expert Determination). Copies of the decision, which consisted of a full comprehensive report and a separate Executive Summary, were also delivered to the World Bank, as required under the Treaty.[105]

---

102 Indus Waters Treaty, supra note 33, Annexure F, para. 9.

103 Salman, *The Baglihar Difference*, supra note 34.

104 S. M. A. Salman & E. Obadia, *The Indus Waters Treaty, the Baglihar Difference and ICSID Administration of the Proceedings*, 23: 2 News from the International Centre for Settlement of Investment Disputes (2006) 1, 14–16, at 14. It should be clarified that ICSID is one of the five institutions that comprise the World Bank Group. The other four are the International Bank for Reconstruction and Development, International Development Association, International Finance Corporation, and Multilateral Investment Guarantee Agency. For more details *see*: http://www.worldbank.org/en/who-we-are.

105 With prior agreement of the two parties, and arrangements with the Neutral Expert, the Bank disclosed to the public on its website the Executive Summary of the Neutral Expert Report. For the Executive Summary, *see* R. Lafitte, *Baglihar Hydroelectric Plant, Expert Determination: Executive Summary* (Lausanne, 12 February 2007), http://siteresources

It should be added that India had continued with the construction of the Dam during the Neutral Expert process,[106] and the project was completed and commissioned in 2008. However, another disagreement arose between the two countries during the initial filling of the Baglihar Dam. Pakistan claimed that the flow of the Chenab River was being affected due to the speedy filling of the Dam. This issue was discussed and resolved at the Permanent Indus Commission. At a meeting in New Delhi in June 2010, Pakistan informed the Commission that it would not raise the matter further as 'India gave the assurance that it will be careful in future, and Pakistan has accepted that in spirit of cooperation and goodwill.'[107]

2.1.1.6.2.2 *The Baglihar 'Difference' within the Indus Waters Treaty Context*

Pakistan claimed in its request to the World Bank that the Baglihar Dam Project did not conform to criteria (a), (c), (e), and (f) of Paragraph 8 of Annexure D to the Treaty. To elaborate, criterion (a) states that the works shall not be able to artificially raise the water level in the operating pool above the full pondage level specified in the design, and Pakistan alleged that the Baglihar Dam did not meet this requirement. Criterion (c) requires the maximum pondage in the operating pool not to exceed twice the pondage required for firm power, and Pakistan claimed that it exceeded twice that level. Further, criterion (e) states that if the conditions at the plant site make a gated spillway necessary, the bottom level of the gates in normal closed position shall be located at the highest level consistent with sound and economical design. On this point, Pakistan claimed that the Baglihar Dam design was not based on correct, rational, and realistic estimates of maximum flood discharge. Lastly, criterion (f) requires that the intakes for the turbines be located at the highest level, consistent with satisfactory and economical construction and operation of the plant as a run-of-the-river plant, but Pakistan considered that the intakes for the turbines were not located at the highest level as mandated.[108]

.worldbank.org/SOUTHASIAEXT/Resources/223546-1171996340255/BagliharSummary .pdf.

106 As indicated above, Pakistan asked the World Bank at the beginning of the process of appointing the Neutral Expert to issue a provisional order to India to halt construction of the dam until the determination of the Neutral Expert. However, the Bank declined, indicating that its role is confined solely to the appointment of the Neutral Expert. Pakistan did not pursue this matter with the Neutral Expert.

107 Statement of Pakistan's Indus Commissioner, cited in G. Parsai, '*India, Pakistan Resolve Baglihar Dam Issue*', The Hindu (1 June 2010), http://www.thehindu.com/news/India-Pakistan-resolve-Baglihar-dam-issue/article16240199.ece.

108 Salman, *The Baglihar Difference*, supra note 34.

2.1.1.6.2.3 *The Neutral Expert Ruling*

The Executive Summary of the Neutral Expert report makes two interesting overarching legal points. First, it states that the rights and obligations of the parties, under the Indus Waters Treaty, had to be read in the light of new technical norms and standards and interpreted so as to permit the fulfilment of the purpose of the Treaty in 'a spirit of goodwill and friendship' taking into account the best and latest practices in the field of construction and operation of hydro-electric plants. Second, it states that the interpretation of the Treaty was guided by the principles of integration and effectiveness to find effect in its whole and to ensure that each of its objects is given the fullest weight and effect when interpreting the rights and obligations thereunder. Those purposes include attaining the most complete and satisfactory utilization of the waters of the Indus River system, and fixing and delimiting the rights and obligations of each party in relation to the other. The ruling of the Neutral Expert dealt with the contested issues under the four criteria discussed above, under six headings.[109]

The first heading concerned the design flood calculation of the maximum amount of water that can reach the Dam. In view of the many uncertainties in flood analysis, the Neutral Expert retained the value proposed by India (16,500 m^3/s), as opposed to the value proposed by Pakistan (14,900 m^3/s) for the peak discharge of the design flood, and further stated that the possibility of increased flooding due to climate change encouraged such a prudent approach.[110]

The second heading pertained to the question of the need for a gated or an ungated spillway. Pakistan considered that a gated spillway was unnecessary because it would allow India to control the flow of the river. However, the Neutral Expert determined that the hydrology, sediment yield, topography, geology, and seismicity of the site warranted a gated spillway. The Expert further added that the analysis of 13,000 existing spillways in the world demonstrated that gates on large spillways were common practice, that an ungated spillway could increase the risk of flooding the upstream shores, and that an elevation of the dam crest, which would prevent such a risk, would be too costly.[111]

The level of the spillway gates was the theme of the third heading. Pakistan was of the view that even if a gated spillway was deemed necessary, the orifice spillway proposed by India had to be re-located at the highest level consistent with the Treaty. The Indian position, in contrast, was that the design of

---

109 For more details, *see id.*

110 *Id.*

111 *Id.*

the chute, sluice and auxiliary spillways, as proposed, was necessary to ensure safe passing of the design flood. The Neutral Expert, agreeing with India, determined that the gated chute spillway on the left wing planned by India, indeed, was at the highest level consistent with sound and economical design and, therefore, satisfactory. However, the Expert emphasized that the outlets that form the sluice spillway, planned by India, should be of the minimum size and located at the highest level. The Neutral Expert also proposed that the outlets be located eight meters lower to ensure protection against upstream flooding. The Neutral Expert, further, pointed out that the Indus Treaty lacked detail on the issue of sedimentation, understandably because it reflected the status of technology on reservoir sedimentation of the 1950s, and affirmed that, consequently, the provision of the Treaty, explicitly referring to sedimentation, acquired a special significance.[112]

The fourth heading concerned the artificial raising of the water level. On this issue, the Neutral Expert concurred with Pakistan's position that the dam crest elevation proposed by India was exaggerated and could be lowered. The Expert further determined that the crest elevation submitted by India at 844.5 m above sea level (a.s.l.), resulting from a freeboard above the full pondage level of 4.50 m was not at the lowest elevation, and that the freeboard should be 3.0 m above the pondage level, leading to a dam crest elevation of 843.0 m a.s.l.[113]

The volume of the maximum pondage was the fifth heading. Pakistan had argued that the value proposed by India exceeded twice the pondage required for firm power. The Neutral Expert, in contrast, determined that the values for maximum pondage stipulated by both India and Pakistan were not in conformity with the criteria laid down in the Treaty and, therefore, fixed a lower value.[114]

Finally, the sixth heading pertained to the level of the power intake. Pakistan had argued that it was not located at the highest level as required by the Treaty. The Neutral Expert agreed with this view and determined that the intake level should be raised by 3 m and fixed it at an elevation of 821 m a.s.l.[115]

No doubt, the Baglihar difference posed major challenges to governance under the Indus Waters Treaty. However, the reactions to its resolution were positive, and both India and Pakistan accepted the decision and claimed victory, emphasizing the areas of the verdict which they believed responded

112 *Id.*
113 *Id.*
114 *Id.*
115 *Id.*

positively to their specific claims. Baglihar, thus, happens to be a fine example of resolution under the terms and conditions of the Indus Waters Treaty of the first difference ever to arise between India and Pakistan.

Indeed, this was the first time in 45 years that the Treaty's provisions on settlement of differences and disputes were tested. Understandably, there was apprehension in all quarters about how the process might unfold. Concerns about whether there would be an agreement that the Baglihar question had reached the stage of a 'difference' and whether an agreement would be reached on a person to serve as a Neutral Expert were on the minds of many. Equally intensified concerns were about how the Neutral Expert would handle the difference, and how the parties would deal with him, and react to his final decision.

As noted above, the World Bank complied sincerely and fairly with its Treaty obligation regarding the appointment of a Neutral Expert.[116] The Expert was able, with the coordinating role of ICSID and full cooperation of the two parties, to handle the process, and to deliver a decision, largely accepted by the two parties.[117] ICSID rules and practice provided guidance on many procedural decisions taken by the World Bank and the Neutral Expert.

Undoubtedly, the Baglihar process set precedents on many aspects. Transparent and fair procedures for the appointment of the Neutral Expert, and for the conduct of the proceedings, were put in place for the first time since the Treaty was concluded in 1960. Those procedures drew considerably from ICSID practice, the United Nations Commission on International Trade arbitration rules, and the World Trade Organization dispute settlement rules.[118] The result of this blend was a comprehensive and unique set of rules and procedures.[119] On the substantive side, the Neutral Expert, relying on the spirit of the Vienna Convention on the Law of Treaties, alluded to the notion that the rights and obligations of the parties under the Treaty should be read in the

116 Concerned about its relationship with India and Pakistan, and the outcome of the Neutral Expert process, the Bank sought at the early stages of the Baglihar process to resolve the difference through mediation. However, Pakistan objected, and the Bank had to continue with the Neutral Expert process.

117 It should be noted that several Pakistani experts, academics and journalists read the decision of the Neutral Expert as a triumph for India and a loss of Pakistan. *See* for example, '*2007: Neutral Expert Gives His Judgement on Baglihar Dam*', Dawn (2 July 2011), https://www.dawn.com/news/640989. There was a general feeling that Pakistan sought resort to the Neutral Expert process too late, after the Baglihar Dam had become a *fait accompli*, which was difficult for the Neutral Expert to decommission or dismantle.

118 For the details of these procedures, *see* Salman & Obadia, supra note 104.

119 *Id.*, at 1.

light of new technical norms and new standards. This would most likely influence future interpretation of the Treaty.[120]

The reference to the Vienna Convention in the interpretation is, indeed, interesting given that neither state is a party to the Vienna Convention. Moreover, only Pakistan is a party to the ICSID Convention. Nonetheless, both endorsed the designation of ICSID as a coordinator, and neither raised concerns to the invocation of the Vienna Convention in connection with the interpretation of the Indus Waters Treaty.

The cooperation of the two parties, including with regards to the financial cost of the process,[121] and their acceptance of the Neutral Expert's decision was the ultimate triumph of the process. All in all, the way the process started in January 2005, and ended in February 2007, attests to the strength and credibility of the Treaty itself, in addition to underscoring the notion of the peaceful settlement of international water disputes.[122]

2.1.1.6.3 The Kishenganga Dispute and Its Arbitration Process

Distantly linked with the Wullar Barrage, another dispute erupted in the context of the construction of the Kishenganga Hydro Electric Power Project (KHEP). This is a 330 MW hydro-electric project that diverts water to the Jhelum River from the Kishenganga River (called Neelum in Pakistan), itself a

120 *Id.*, at 15.

121 The financial cost of the process, and how it was shouldered, needs brief discussion. As indicated above, under Annexure F of the Treaty, each of the two parties was required to pay to the Bank, once the Treaty entered into force, the sum of US$5,000. The Bank would hold this amount, together with any income therefrom, in a trust to pay the remuneration of the Neutral Expert and any assistance he may need. The US$10,000 paid by the two parties in 1960, and held by the World Bank in a trust fund, had reached over US$100,000 in 2005 when the Neutral Expert was appointed, as a result of the investment of the original amount. The balance in the trust fund covered the initial expenses incurred to start the Neutral Expert process. The Treaty authorizes the Bank to ask the parties to pay in equal shares any amount required to cover the cost of the process after depleting the amount held by the Bank in the trust fund. The parties agreed, and paid in equal shares the amounts so requested by the Bank. The fund was left after the process was completed with the amount (close to US$105,000) to cover the cost of the process of any future Neutral Expert. The Neutral Expert also ruled that each party would bear its own expenses of the process, a further indication that the determination meant that no party really lost. The Bank decided that the cost of its staff time would be borne by the Bank, only the travel costs of the ICSID staff (and not the other Bank staff), in connection with the meetings planned already by the Neutral Expert, would be reimbursed from the Indus fund held by the Bank. This resulted in a transparent and fair burden sharing of the cost of the whole process, and the Bank shared a part of that cost as a result of its Treaty-specified role and obligations, and did not pass it to the fund it held, or to the two parties.

122 *See* Salman, *The Baglihar Difference*, supra note 34, at 116.

Jhelum tributary. Pakistan instituted an arbitral proceeding at the Permanent Court of Arbitration (PCA),[123] on 17 May 2010, against India, with two main issues. The first issue pertained to whether or not India's proposed diversion of the Kishenganga River into another tributary, a central element of the KHEP, breached India's legal obligations to Pakistan under the Indus Waters Treaty, as interpreted and applied in accordance with international law, including India's obligations under Article III (2) (to let all the waters of the Western Rivers flow and to not interfere with those waters) and Article IV (6) (maintain natural channels). The second issue pertained to whether under the Indus Waters Treaty, India may deplete or bring the reservoir level of a run-of-the-river plant below Dead Storage Level (DSL) under any circumstance, except in the case of an unforeseen emergency.[124]

2.1.1.6.3.1 *The Kishenganga Dispute and the Court of Arbitration Ruling*

The PC gave a partial award on the Kishenganga dispute on 18 February 2013 and its final award on 20 December 2013.[125] The Final Award was unanimous. It specified that, in the operation of the KHEP, (1) subject to paragraph (2) below, India had to release a minimum flow of 9 m^3s^{-1} (nine cubic meters per second) into the Kishenganga River below the KHEP at all times, at which the daily average flow in the River immediately upstream of the KHEP meets or exceeds 9 m^3s^{-1} and (2) any time the daily average flow in the Kishenganga River immediately upstream of the KHEP was less than 9 m^3s^{-1}, India had to release 100% of the daily average flow immediately upstream of the KHEP into the Kishenganga River below the KHEP. It further specified that, seven years after the diversion of water from the Kishenganga River for power generation

123 The panel of the Court of Arbitration was composed of six lawyers and an engineer: Judge Stephen M. Schwebel (Chairman); Sir Franklin Berman KCMG QC; Professor Howard S. Wheater, FREng; Professor Lucius Caflisch; Professor Jan Paulsson; Judge Bruno Simma; and H. E. Judge Peter Tomka.

124 *See* the Permanent Court of Arbitration (PCA), *In the matter of the Indus Waters Kishenganga Arbitration* (Pakistan v. India), Final Award, 20 December 2013. Text of the Award accessible at the PCA website, available at: Partial Award (18 February 2013), https://www.pcacases.com/web/sendAttach/1681; Final Award, https://www.pcacases.com/web/sendAttach/48.

125 Id. For a detailed discussion of the case *see* K. Uprety, '*The Kishenganga Arbitration: Reviving the Indus Treaty and Managing Transboundary Hydropolitics*', 14 Chinese Journal of International Law (2015), 497–543; *see also* B-O. Magsig, *International Water Law and the Quest for Common Security* (London: Routledge, 2015) at 187–189.

by the KHEP, either party could seek reconsideration of the minimum flow specified above through the PIC and the mechanism of the Indus Treaty.[126]

Not surprisingly, for an issue so deeply tied with geo-politics, coupled with historical acrimony between the two countries, the reactions about the final Award were inevitably mixed. Indeed, there was ample joy for victory and enough sadness for defeat in both countries. In each country, there was one side that referred to the verdict as having saved sovereignty and another side as having compromised vital national interests. Moreover, the fickle favor of some newspapers from both countries swept from one view to another, providing readers a kaleidoscope of disparate views, leaving most of them confused. However, to draw a balanced conclusion about the value of the arbitral award, all this should be reduced to perspective, and one needs to appreciate not only the perceptional, but also the substantive, aspects of its causality and effects. Besides the internal inherent political considerations and resulting biases, one important reason for the mixed reactions was, understandably, the PCA's efforts to take a middle path attempting to strike a balance between the environmental concerns and the energy requirements of the two countries on the one hand, and between their rights and duties spelled out in the Treaty, on the other.

2.1.1.6.3.2 *Point-Counterpoint Regarding the Award on Kishenganga*

However disparate the views may have been, the Award, nonetheless, was considered a win-win for both countries. It enabled India (with some significant changes) to proceed with developing hydropower projects on the Jhelum and Chenab Rivers, and restored, if not redefined, Pakistan's water share on the Indus, Jhelum and Chenab Rivers.

From a techno-legal perspective, for India, the Award more specifically means that it can continue to develop its hydropower projects on the Chenab and Jhelum Rivers, but it must respect the Treaty defined limits on storage and use methods other than the construction of low gates to flush silt. The Award, having banned the use of drawdown flushing in all future projects (an interpretation which is completely opposite to the Baglihar ruling), essentially means that all the new projects will either have to survive with shorter life, or will have to use a new technology to manage the massive sedimentation load that often kills dams and reservoirs. In this context, it may be useful to recall that all the major rivers in Jammu and Kashmir and their tributaries have

126 PCA, *id.*, p. 43. For a detailed analysis, *see* Uprety, *id.; see also* M. Tignino, '*Le Fleuve Indus et Ses Usages: L'arbitrage Relatif Aux Eaux du Fleuve Kishenganga*', LX Annuaire Français de droit International (2014) 519–542.

massively silted flows, and the Chenab River, the major power house of the state, suffers from crisis-level sediment loads. Therefore, the challenge is clear and quite substantial for India. It must be more creative and imaginative in the way in which it deals with silt management, as well as environmental flows.

For Pakistan, the Award meant that due to the construction of the KHEP, the flow of water for the Neelum Jhelum Hydro Electric Project (in Pakistan) will decrease. Although this will reduce annual energy generation, Pakistan can now reasonably claim that basic environmental flows be restored on the Ravi and Sutlej Rivers. Further, Pakistan will not be threatened by the development of a large amount of easy-to-manipulate storage by India on the Jhelum and Chenab Rivers. Most importantly, for both countries, a series of domestic legal and policy changes will have to be made about their hydro development, allocation, and management systems and practices.

From an international legal perspective, the Award is a landmark for governance of shared water resources. Indeed, it has provided a relatively clearer response to a multitude of important questions on the relevance of the Indus Treaty, the models of development adopted by building large dams and reservoirs for hydroelectric power with environmental consequences, the application of international environmental obligations, and the adequacy of existing international courts and tribunals and their procedures to settle complex water disputes. From an internationalist's angle, moreover, the Award is also historic because it revives the Indus Treaty as a central and viable instrument for cooperation on the use of the waters of the Indus Basin.[127]

A noteworthy aspect of the Award is its forward-looking approach. As noted above, the Treaty was based on the general state of knowledge, technology, and climate of opinion prevalent at the time of its negotiation, and thus, is limited to engineering of the 1950s. At that time, concepts such as environmental impact assessments, minimum flows, or environmental flows, and issues such as climate change were not very common, or perhaps even heard of. Yet, the Award, thanks to the broad-mindedness of the judges, remarkably has provided interpretation of several of these concepts and issues through a modern lens, showing concerns for new developments, and ensuring the applicability of balancing treaty provisions.

A further notable point emanating from these proceedings is the emergence of the claim to customary status of the precautionary principle, and the question of its status in international law. On this question, the PCA emphasized that it did not consider it appropriate, and certainly not necessary, for it to

127 *See* generally, B. Desai & B. K. Sidhu, '*The Kishenganga Final Award: Is the Indus Waters Treaty at the Crossroads?*', 49 Political and Economic Weekly (15 February 2014).

adopt a precautionary approach and to assume the role of a policymaker in determining the balance between acceptable environmental change and other priorities, or to permit environmental considerations to override the balance of other rights and obligations. The PCA alluded to the contentious nature of the principle by indicating that it belonged in the realm of policy.[128] Indeed, this happened after ample discussions about the environmental concerns against water security, moving from a narrow discussion on the definition of security to one that explored the complex interface between the environment and security.

Amid the satisfactions, dissatisfactions, skepticism, and interesting legal enunciations revolving around the Award, there are also water experts like Desai and Sidhu who, convinced by practicality and realism, stressed that

> to better harness the hydro potential of the shared watercourses in the Indus basin, both countries will have to learn from world history and consider joint design and implementation of hydro power projects that take a holistic hydrological view and maintain the environmental integrity of the entire Indus basin without compromising the developmental needs of both the riparians.[129]

Similar insights have been shared by other water experts such as Subramanian, Brown and Wolf, who noted that 'cooperation promises substantial economic benefits, as well, including access to external markets, improved management and coordinated operation of water infrastructure, and optimal location of infrastructure, to name a few.'[130] Indeed, only political sagacity and sensitivity

---

128 For a brief discussion, *see* O. W. Pedersen, *'From Abundance to Indeterminacy: The Precautionary Principle and Its Two Camps of Custom'*, 3:2 Transnational Environmental Law (2014) 323–339.

129 Desai & Sidhu, supra note 127.

130 These authors further noted that 'additionally, joint development of a shared river can increase the sustainability of the resource and help the needs and interests of all countries involved.' *See* for instance, A. Subramanian et al., *'Understanding and Overcoming Risks to Cooperation Along Transboundary Rivers'*, 16 Water Policy (2014) 824–843, at 825. They again noted that 'beyond the river benefits' can also be created, such as opportunities for regional cooperation over labor, markets, and infrastructure, not directly related to the river (citing Claudia Sadoff and David Grey). Similar type of conclusion has been made by other experts who propose a number of enabling conditions for the Indus, including the existence and recognition of interdependency among contending stakeholders, focus on framing mutual interests via joint fact finding, and creating mutual benefits, formation of a joint body to monitor agreements and address new problems as they emerge. *See* E. Choudhury & S. Islam, *'Nature of Transboundary Water Conflicts:*

towards the legacy of common heritage can help these countries overcome their animosity and take an open view of cooperation on the shared Indus waters.

2.1.1.6.4 The Continued Saga of the Indus Differences and Disputes

It seems that the saga of the Indus waters disputes never actually ends. It only twists and turns around. India and Pakistan again requested, in November 2016, the World Bank's assistance in deciding on several technical issues pertaining to the construction of the above-discussed Kishenganga Hydroelectric Project (being built by India on a tributary of the Jhelum River), and the Ratle Hydropower Project, an 850 megawatts run-of-river power plant (being built by India on a tributary of the Chenab River in the Indian State of Jammu and Kashmir).[131]

2.1.1.6.4.1 *The Discord*

The two countries' disagreement on the construction of the two dams centers on whether or not the technical design features of the two hydroelectric plants conform with the provisions of the Treaty. This time around, regarding the Kishenganga specifically, Pakistan wants to counter India on the 'design' aspects of the dam, through a court of arbitration on grounds that the design was detrimental to Pakistan's interests. It also claims that the pondage of the project, at 7.5 million cubic meters, is excessive, and that it should not exceed one million cubic meters. Pakistan further wants India to raise the intakes by up to four meters and spillways up to nine meters in height.[132]

With regards to the Ratle Hydropower Project plant, for which construction started in June 2013, with the first power generation expected in 2018, Pakistan voiced concerns over the Project design. It raised concerns over the proposed lower spillways for sediment management, which it alleges could lead to flooding, and was of the view that higher spillways should be established instead of lower ones.[133]

Issues of Complexity and the Enabling Conditions for Negotiated Cooperation', 155:1 Journal of Contemporary Water Research & Education (July 2015) 43–52, at 47–49.

131 *See 'Ratle Hydroelectric Power Plant, Jammu and Kashmir*', Power Technology (undated), https://www.power-technology.com/projects/ratle-hydroelectric-power-plant-jammu-and-kashmir/.

132 '*World Bank Asks India, Pakistan to Agree to Mediation on Indus Waters Treaty*', The Economic Times (11 November 2016). *See also 'World Bank Halts Parallel Processes on India-Pakistan Hydel Projects*', The Economic Times (14 December 2016).

133 *See 'World Bank Asks India', id.*

Pakistan claims that, construction of the Ratle hydropower plant on the Chenab River under its existing objectionable design will reduce the water flow of the Chenab River at Head Marala by 40%, which will be detrimental to irrigation in Central Punjab in Pakistan. Note that India has awarded the contract of the Rattle Project to a private company that will run the project on a BOT (build, operate and transfer) basis for 35 years before handing over the project to India. This dam will be three times larger than the Baglihar hydropower dam. India has already carved out a plan to generate 32,000 MW of electricity on Pakistan's Western Rivers that will enable New Delhi to regulate the water flows that are destined to reach Pakistan.[134]

Pakistan also wants India to maintain free board at one meter, whereas India wants to keep it at two meters. In addition, India wants to keep the pondage of 24 million cubic meters, but Pakistan wants a pondage of 8 million cubic meters. Moreover, Pakistan wants the intake of the project to be raised by up to 8.8 meters, and it spillways be raised by up to 20 meters.[135]

2.1.1.6.4.2 *The Parties' Requests to the World Bank*

Pakistan asked the World Bank to facilitate setting up a court of arbitration to look into its concerns about the designs of the two hydroelectric power projects. India asked for the appointment of a Neutral Expert for the same purpose. These requests came after the Permanent Indus Commission had been engaged in discussions on the matter for some time. During several months prior to December 12, 2016, the World Bank sought to fulfil its procedural obligations with respect to both the court of arbitration and the Neutral Expert. Thus, two parallel processes to adjudicate technical differences between India and Pakistan (appointing a Neutral Expert as demanded by India, and establishing a court of arbitration as demanded by Pakistan), had been requested. India had been against the duality of process, arguing that they would be unworkable.[136]

2.1.1.6.4.3 *The World Bank's Initial Decision*

It is important to recall that the Treaty does not empower the World Bank to choose whether one procedure should take precedence over the other. Instead, the Treaty determines the mechanism to resolve the issue based on the nature

---

134 K. Mustafa, '*India Completes Kishenganga Project with Faulty Design*', The News International (Karachi) (28 November 2017).

135 K. Mustafa, '*Pak-India Talks on Kishenganga and Ratle Hydropower Projects Fail*', The News International (Karachi) (1 July 2016).

136 '*World Bank Asks India*', supra note 132; *see also* '*World Bank Halts Parallel Processes*', supra note 132.

of the issue at variance between the two parties. The Bank agreed to establish the two processes demanded by the two parties, and at the same time actively encouraged both countries to agree amicably on a mechanism to address the issues.[137]

In response to their separate proceedings initiated under the Indus Waters Treaty, on 11 November 2016, the World Bank suggested that India and Pakistan should agree on mediation to resolve issues regarding the two dams. However, concurrently, the World Bank also held a drawing of lots at its headquarters in Washington, DC to determine who will appoint the three umpires to sit on the court of arbitration that Pakistan has requested. Following on India's request, it also proposed the names of three potential candidates for appointment as a Neutral Expert.[138]

2.1.1.6.4.4 *The World Bank's Revised Decision*

On 14 December 2016, the World Bank again wrote to both governments announcing its decision to halt the two parallel processes. It realized that the processes initiated by the respective countries were advancing at the same time, creating the risk of contradictory outcomes that could potentially endanger the Treaty, and the two processes, as well as the role of the World Bank itself.[139] The World Bank asked both countries to try to reach consensus on either the mechanism of the Neutral Expert, or of the court of arbitration for the resolution of the issues pertaining to the said projects.

Recall that the Indus Waters Treaty, as discussed above, lays down detailed procedures and criteria for the appointment of the Neutral Expert, as well as the establishment of a court of arbitration. Unless the two parties agree to adopt procedures different from those set forth in the Treaty, the Bank has no authority to change or adapt these procedures.

Amid this confusion and hesitation, the World Bank held further talks with both India and Pakistan separately to find a way out of the two requested procedures and the resulting dilemma. Consequently, the Bank appointed a third party, whose task, it was explained, is to assist the two countries to build a road map for mediation of the issues surrounding the two power plants.[140]

---

137 *Id.*

138 *See* World Bank, '*World Bank Urges Mediation for India, Pakistan over Indus*', Press Release (10 November 2016), http://www.worldbank.org/en/news/press-release/2016/11/10/world-bank-urges-mediation-for-india-pakistan-over-indus. It should be noted that neither of the two plants is being financed by the Bank.

139 *Id.*

140 *See* World Bank, '*World Bank Declares Pause to Protect Indus Waters Treaty*', Press Release (12 December 2016), http://www.worldbank.org/en/news/press-release/2016/12/12/world

2.1.1.6.4.5 *The World Bank Approach Critiqued*

Whether under the provisions of the Indus Waters Treaty two processes can simultaneously be initiated is indeed quite debatable; and is no doubt a matter for academics and *opinio juris* to ponder. However, one thing is certain, the process has not been properly and appropriately managed by the World Bank. Had the parties gone ahead with the initial recommendation, there was the possibility for the outcome to have triggered two separate and possibly contradictory rulings (impossible to implement and prone to furthering the conflict). Even if the dual process was aborted, the announcement of the Bank's original decision was too hasty, which, one could say, has now put one or the other country in a weak position for any resolution of this specific dispute in the future.

Moreover, the halting by the World Bank of the process for such a long period of time, and seeking instead to establish a mediation process, does not, in the view of the authors of this monograph, comport with the Indus Waters Treaty, and the role of the Bank specified therein. As discussed above, the World Bank did recommend to the two parties resolution of the Baglihar difference through mediation. However, when Pakistan rejected this proposal, the Bank proceeded without delay with the appointment of the Neutral Expert. In the current cases of Kishenganga and Ratle, the difference/dispute resolution process, at the time of completing this monograph, is still in limbo. The World Bank has neither followed the provisions of the Treaty, nor succeeded in getting the two parties to agree to mediation. Time is clearly not on the side of Pakistan, as the two plants are poised to become a *fait accompli* soon.

-bank-declares-pause-protect-indus-water-treaty. The announcement halted the appointment of the Neutral Expert, as requested by India, and the establishment of a court of arbitration, as requested by Pakistan, to resolve issues regarding the two hydroelectric power plants under construction by India along the Indus rivers system. Processes initiated by the respective country were advancing at the same time, creating a risk of contradictory outcomes that could potentially endanger the Treaty. While making the announcement, the World Bank President made the following statement: 'We are announcing this pause to protect the Indus Waters Treaty and to help India and Pakistan consider alternative approaches to resolving conflicting interests under the Treaty and its application to two hydroelectric power plants.... This is an opportunity for the two countries to begin to resolve the issue in an amicable manner and in line with the spirit of the treaty rather than pursuing concurrent processes that could make the treaty unworkable over time. I would hope that the two countries will come to an agreement by the end of January.'

2.1.1.7 *Effects of the Indus Waters Treaty on National Water Governance*

While the conclusion of the Indus Waters Treaty resolved a major international crisis between India and Pakistan, the Treaty also had major impacts on the national water governance within the territory of each country. Both countries had to take new measures to deal with the impact of the Treaty on their national/internal sharing and management arrangements of their respective rivers and river waters.

2.1.1.7.1 Inter-province Water Sharing Issues in Pakistan

As discussed above, Pakistan built a number of water infrastructure projects as a result of the Indus Waters Treaty. These projects included the storage reservoirs at Chashma (on the Indus) and Mangla (on the Jhelum), in addition to six new head works and seven large inter-river link channels in 1970, and the Tarbela Dam in 1976 (on the Indus). However, between 1971 and 1991, there was no formal system within Pakistan that quantified water allocated from the Indus River to any of the four provinces of Balochistan, Punjab, Sindh, and the North-West Frontier. The federal government addressed the issue of water security of the four provinces by allotting the water from its Western Rivers on an *ad hoc* basis for each crop season.[141] A formal arrangement for the allocation of waters of the Indus system was, therefore, needed in Pakistan. For that purpose, an Indus System Waters Apportionment Accord was concluded in 1991, which fixed the quantum of water allocated among the four provinces, established a system for future allocations, and enabled the provinces to determine the location of water storage projects based on their share.[142]

The Accord essentially was designed to address and try to ensure water security of the provinces, as demanded by each of them. It also provided for the establishment of an Indus River System Authority, headquartered in Lahore, with representation from the four provinces. Operationalized in 1993, the Authority was mandated to regulate the distribution of water among provinces, to ensure that each province gets its allotted share, and to facilitate agreements on equitable inter-province allocations. Admittedly, the Authority has not been able to resolve all conflicts. The dispute between Sindh and Punjab, for instance, is still pending, as the former demands its share based on the formula in the Accord, while the latter's demands are based on historical

---

141 See K. Uprety & S. M. A. Salman, '*Legal Aspects of Sharing and Management of Transboundary Waters in South Asia: Preventing Conflicts and Promoting Cooperation*', 56 Hydrological Science Journal (2011) 641–661.

142 The 1991 Water Apportionment Accord is on file with authors. For more discussion of the Accord, *see* Uprety and Salman, *id.*

usage.[143] However, the forum for discussions provided by the Authority has certainly been, to a certain extent, a deterrent to any serious and unmanageable inter-province conflicts.

2.1.1.7.2 Inter-state Water Sharing Issues in India: The Punjab-Haryana Dispute

As discussed above, the Indus Waters Treaty, under which both India and Pakistan were allowed unrestricted use of three rivers each, allocated to India the Eastern Rivers (Sutlej, Beas, and Ravi). Once the treaty was signed in 1960, the waters from these three rivers were shared between Punjab, Delhi, and Jammu and Kashmir. In 1966, Punjab was re-organized and the state of Haryana was created out of it. As a successor state, Haryana was eligible to receive a share of Punjab's river waters. The river Yamuna (whose course took it through undivided Punjab, but now flowed only in Haryana) was never considered a part of this arrangement.[144]

Predictably, the sharing of river waters became a bone of contention between Punjab and Haryana, as it is with other inter-provincial rivers.[145] In 1976, then Prime Minister Indira Gandhi intervened and directed that of the available 15.2 million acre-feet (MAF) (18,748,924,018 cubic meters) of water from the three rivers, Punjab and Haryana would each receive 3.5 MAF (4,317,186,452 cubic meters).[146] The intervention was certainly bold and decisive, but with that, the authors think, the seeds of trouble were also sown.

---

143 *Id.*

144 *'Punjab Must Share Water with Haryana: Supreme Court'*, The Logical Indian (11 November 2016).

145 In this context, it should be noted that under the federal structure of India, water is a state matter, with a limited, defined role for each government. Seventeen out of India's eighteen major rivers are shared by two or more states. The competing demands of states thus lead to protracted difficult disputes, and in some cases, even lead to non-resolution. For detailed analysis, see S. M. A. Salman, *'Inter-states Water Disputes in India: An Analysis of the Settlement Process'*, 4:3 Water Policy (2002) 223–237.

146 It is worth noting that in 1977, the design of the Sutlej Yamuna Canal (SYC) was finalized and the first notice for land acquisition to build it was issued. However, a group of the Akali Dal (Dharam Yudh Morcha) in 1982 opposed its construction. This issue was resolved under the Punjab Accord, which ended the three-year Sikh confrontation with the Indian government. Paragraph 9 of the Accord, entitled 'Sharing of River Waters', states as follows:

> 9.1 The farmers of Punjab, Haryana and Rajasthan will continue to get water not less than what they are using from the Ravi Beas system as on 1.7.85. Waters used for consumptive purposes will also remain unaffected. Quantum of usage shall be verified by the Tribunal referred to in Para 9.2 below.
>
> 9.2 The claim of Punjab and Haryana regarding the shares in their remaining waters will be referred for adjudication to a Tribunal to be presided over by a Supreme Court Judge. The decision of this Tribunal will be rendered within six months and would be

Already in 1979, Haryana had approached the Supreme Court and asked for an order to implement the allocation Premier Gandhi's intervention had set. Punjab filed a civil suit at the Supreme Court a few months later, challenging that request. In 2002, the Supreme Court issued a directive to the Punjab government to complete the canal.[147] To counter this, the then-chief minister of Punjab helmed the Punjab Termination of Waters Agreement Act, 2004, which was unanimously adopted by the Punjab assembly. The Act annulled all earlier accords and awards on the apportionment of river waters between Punjab, Haryana, and Rajasthan, and provided statutory protection for the first time to the water already flowing to Rajasthan and Haryana.[148]

The 2004 Punjab Termination of Waters Agreement Act was referred, subsequent to its issuance, to the Supreme Court by the President of India.[149] The

---

binding on both parties. All legal and constitutional steps required in this respect shall be taken immediately.

9.3 The construction of SYL Canal shall continue. The Canal shall be completed by August 15, 1986.

Also, pursuant to the Accord, the Inter-State River Water Disputes Act 1956 (ISRWD Act) was amended and a three-member Ravi and Beas Waters Tribunal was set up in April 1986 to verify and adjudicate the matters specified in paragraphs 9.1 and 9.2 respectively. The Tribunal gave its report on 31 January 1987, which was forwarded to the states on 20 May 1987. References under Section 5(3) of the ISRWD Act, of Punjab, Haryana and Rajasthan and Central governments seeking some explanation/guidance on the report, were forwarded to the Tribunal on 19 August 1987 and are under their consideration. *See* Government of India, Ministry of Water Resources, River Development and Ganga Rejuvenation website, http://mowr.gov.in.

147 The Supreme Court's directive to the Punjab government was to complete construction of the long-pending Sutlej-Yamuna Link (SYL) canal within one year.

148 *See 'President Seeks SC View on SYL Row'*, Rediff News (23 July 2004), http://www.rediff.com/news/2004/jul/22syl.htm.

149 Faced with a raging inter-state row after Punjab annulled all river water sharing agreements with neighboring states, the Centre (Union Government) decided to refer the controversial measure to the Supreme Court. The central government's move came ten days after the Punjab assembly passed the law that has been stoutly opposed by Haryana, Rajasthan, and Himachal Pradesh, which had asked the Centre to take immediate steps to resolve the crisis. The Centre had on July 15 approached the Supreme Court for fresh directions on the construction of the SYL Canal following Punjab's unilateral decision on July 12 to scrap its river water sharing agreements with neighboring states. In seeking the Supreme Court's opinion on this decision by Punjab, the President, raised the four questions:

1. Are the Punjab Termination of Agreements Act, 2004 and the provisions thereof in accordance with the provisions of the Constitution of India?
2. Are the Punjab Termination of Agreements Act, 2004 and the provisions thereof in accordance with the provisions of Section 14 of the Inter-State Water Disputes Act, 1956, Section 78 of the Punjab Reorganization Act, 1966 and the Notification dated 24 March 1976 issued thereunder?

Central government's perspective was that Punjab's enactment of this act violated two earlier Supreme Court judgments. Now, Haryana has petitioned the Court to expedite the case. The decision is pending.

Thus, the conclusion of the Indus Waters Treaty by India and Pakistan in 1960 has been having major impacts and repercussions on inter-provincial water allocation in each country.

2.1.1.8 *Partial Observations*

Despite the series of contentions, complications, and conflicts, overall, the Indus Waters Treaty should still be recognized as a success story.[150] Also, as pointed out by a scholar, 'When a treaty is negotiated over ten years and is approved and signed at the highest level, it must be presumed that it was the best outcome that was possible under the given circumstances.'[151] Indeed, in addition to successfully halting a bitter dispute by dividing the rivers of the Basin, it has survived continual regional hostility, including two wars between

---

3. Did the State of Punjab validly terminate the agreement dated 31 December 1981 and all other agreements relating to the Ravi Beas waters, and is it discharged from its obligation under the said agreement(s)?
4. Finally, in view of the provisions of the Act, is the State of Punjab discharged from its obligations flowing from the judgment and decree dated 15 January 2002 and the judgment and order dated 4 June 2004 of the Supreme Court of India?

See, *President Seeks SC View on SYL Row, id.*

150 W. Wheeler, '*The Water's Edge*', GOOD Magazine (13 July 2009). However, there are also some authors who question the efficacy of the Indus Waters Treaty. Indeed, its efficacy has started to come into question 'amidst imperatives of the climate change affecting the water reserves and continuing political disputes between India and Pakistan, Kashmir in particular,' *See* A. Kamal, 'An Overview of the Seminar on Water Security', Margalla Papers 2011, Special Edition, Vol. XV, No. 1, *National Defence University* (2011) ii–viii, at iii, http://www.ndu.edu.pk/issra/issra_pub/articles/margalla-paper/Margalla-Papers-SE-2011/Margalla-Papers-2011-Special-Edition.pdf. Also, some authors noted that the Indus Treaty is considered as a 'suboptimal solution' to the management of the Indus. *See* S. Akhtar, 'Quest for Re-Interpreting the Indus Waters Treaty: Pakistan's Dilemma', Margalla Papers, Special Edition, Vol. XV, No. 1, *National Defence University* (2011) 15–46, at 24, http://www.ndu.edu.pk/issra/issra_pub/articles/margalla-paper/Margalla-Papers-SE-2011/02-Quest-for-Re-interpreting.pdf.

151 R. R. Iyer, '*Hydro-Diplomacy for Hydro-Harmony*', in G. Pangare (ed.), *Hydro Diplomacy. Sharing Water Across Borders* (New Delhi: Academic Foundation, 2014) 75–84, at 76. Gopalkrishna Gandhi refers to the story of the Indus Treaty as an example of 'calibrated grace, a measured graciousness, a calculated reposting of faith by both sides.' *See* G. Gandhi, '*Hydro-Wisdom Must Back Hydro-Diplomacy*', in Pangare, *id.*, 9–16, at 10. *See also*, for some lessons learnt in conflict resolution, A. T. Wolf & J. T. Newton, *Case Study of Transboundary Dispute Resolution: the Indus Waters Treaty*, https://www.researchgate.net/publication/251497725_Case_Study_of_Transboundary_Dispute_Resolution_the_Indus_Water_Treaty.

India and Pakistan. Implementing the regime has certainly been a difficult exercise, but thanks largely to the Treaty's built-in mechanisms, the parties have been able to maintain its overall spirit despite the frequent upheavals in their bilateral relations. The resolution of the Baglihar difference, and the first Kishenganga dispute, underscores this conclusion. Nonetheless, it cannot be ignored that since China and Afghanistan, both riparians, are not signatories to the Treaty, their positions regarding its normative provisions remain unclear, restraining anyone from forecasting the Treaty's long-term impact.

2.1.2 The Ganges River System

The Ganges River originates in the Himalayas in Nepal and China. After flowing southeast through India, where it drains roughly 30% of the country, it continues through Bangladesh (1,560 miles). The Brahmaputra River originates in the Himalayas (Yarlung Zangbo in Tibet), and links China, India and Bangladesh (1,800 miles). It joins the Ganges near the town of Goalanda in Bangladesh, from which point onward the combined flow is known as the Padma River. Three major tributaries originating in Bhutan join the Brahmaputra River in India.[152] Farther downstream, the River is joined by the Meghna River at Chandpur (Bangladesh) before emptying into the Bay of Bengal.[153]

The Ganges River has also been a source of a bitter dispute amongst its riparians. Tensions between Bangladesh and India over water sharing are prolonged due to the continually increasing demands for industrial and irrigation uses in the Indian state of West Bengal.[154] Having failed to find a long-term solution over several fragmented issues on the tributaries of the Ganges, Nepal and India continue to argue and clamor for solutions to secure an adequate quantum of water each for what it perceives as its needs and entitlement.

The genesis of attempts at formal water cooperation along the Ganges Basin goes back to 29 April 1875, the date of an Agreement between the then British government and the Sindh state for regulating the supply of water for irrigation from the Western Jumna Canal (amended on 24 July 1892). This was followed by another agreement between the British government and the Patiala state, on 29 August 1893, regarding the Sirsa branch of that canal. Since then, a number of bilateral instruments have been concluded among the riparian countries.

---

152 These rivers are the Beki, the Raidak and the Manas.

153 Fifty-eight percent of the Ganges Basin falls in India; 20% in China; 9% in Nepal; 7% in Bangladesh; 2% in Bhutan; 4% in disputed areas between China and India; and 1% in Myanmar; *see Atlas of International Freshwater Agreements,* supra note 25, at 59.

154 *See* generally, B. M. Abbas, *The Ganges Water Dispute* (New Delhi: University Press Ltd., 1982).

There are two sets of agreements pertaining to the Ganges Basin. The first set comprise the 1920 agreement between Nepal and India (then the British Empire) for the Sarada Barrage on the Mahakali River, the 1954 agreement on the Kosi Project, the 1959 agreement on the Gandak Irrigation and Power Project, the 1991 MoU for the construction of the Tanakpur Barrage, and the 1996 treaty concerning the integrated development of the Mahakali River between Nepal and India. Then, there is the 1977 agreement on sharing of the Ganges waters and on augmenting its flows, the two MoUs in 1982 and 1985 pertaining to the Ganges waters, and the 1996 treaty on sharing the Ganges waters at Farakka between Bangladesh and India.[155] Hence, one set, between India and Bangladesh deals with the operation of Farakka Barrage and water sharing in the lower basin. Another set, between India and Nepal, addresses river governance, power generation, water sharing and irrigation on the tributaries of the Ganges in the upper basin.

2.1.2.1 *India–Bangladesh Regime for the Ganges River*

In 1951, India made public its intention to build a barrage at the head of the Ganges River Delta in West Bengal (the Farakka Barrage), 11 miles upstream from the border with East Pakistan (now Bangladesh).[156] Construction began in 1961 and the Barrage became operational in 1975. Because it diverted water into a canal for irrigation and then into a channel of the Hooghly River (flowing into Kolkata) and prevented water from flowing into Bangladesh, allegedly damaging its water table, the Barrage became a source of acute tension between the two countries.[157]

---

155 India has been planning since 2000 a 'National River Linking Project' which involves connecting 37 rivers, most of them beginning in the Himalayan Mountains, from North to West and South. If built, it would be one of the largest inter-basin transfer projects in the world. For details, http://iasscore.in/national-issues/national-river-linking-project (visited 29 May 2018); *see also* A. R. M. Khalid, '*The Interlinking of Rivers Project in India and International Water Law: An Overview*', 3:2 Chinese Journal of International Law (2004) 553–570.

156 Abbas, supra note 154. For an interesting discussion, *see also* K. A. Thomas, '*The River-border Complex: A Border-integrated Approach to Transboundary River Governance Illustrated by the Ganges River and Indo Bangladeshi Border*', 42:1 Water International (2017) 34–53.

157 Some observers consider that the issue raised by Bangladesh was technical in nature and affected the economic fate of the whole of eastern India, while the effects on Bangladesh only concerned irrigation benefits. Also, such observers refuse to consider the Ganges as an international river because more than 90% of its course flows through Indian Territory. *See* for instance, D. K. Kapoor, *International Law and Human Rights* (India: Central Law Agency, 14th ed., 2002), at 237–238.

Concurrent to this controversy, India and Bangladesh had, in 1972, formalized an instrument referred to as the 'Statute of the Indo-Bangladesh Joint Rivers Commission' with the view to working together in harnessing the 54 rivers common to both countries for the benefit of their peoples.[158] However, the Statute, due to its general coverage, did not include a specific provision obligating India to adapt the operation of the Farakka Barrage, which disappointed Bangladesh. In 1976, it sponsored a resolution at the United Nations calling on India to consider the interests of Bangladesh in the operation of the Farakka Barrage.[159] The resolution failed to pass, but the General Assembly issued a statement of consensus calling on the parties to resolve the issue peacefully.[160]

Indeed, the consensus statement adopted by the United Nations General Assembly on 26 November 1976, proved to be a jump-starter to the Indo-Bangladesh negotiations over the Ganges. The first ministerial level meeting between the two countries was held in December 1976, in Dhaka, and continued in January 1977 in New Delhi.

However, the political change that resulted from the elections in India in March 1977 proved more important to the Ganges dispute. The Congress Party was voted out of office, and the Janata party came to power, with Morarji Desai as Prime Minister. The Janata party was not shackled by previous positions. It wanted to open a new chapter in relations with Bangladesh, and bearing in mind the perceived embarrassment emanating from the United Nations Consensus Statement, it moved quickly in the direction of reaching an agreement with Bangladesh.

After a series of ministerial level meetings and lengthy negotiations, the two parties were finally able to define the issues for an agreement: a temporary arrangement for sharing the waters of the Ganges while a long-term solution for augmenting its flow during the dry season was being sought. An agreement incorporating those two principles and specifying the share of each country was initialed on 30 September 1977, and was signed on 5 November 1977, in Dhaka, by the Minister of Agriculture and Irrigation on behalf of India, and by a member of the President's Council of Advisers in charge of the Ministry

158 For a brief discussion, on the Statute of the Joint Rivers Commission *see* Salman & Uprety, *Conflict and Cooperation*, supra note 30, at 134–135.

159 For detail on the UN Role, *see* Salman & Uprety, *id.*, at 142–148.

160 Interestingly, each of the two parties relied heavily, and almost equally, on the Helsinki Rules, issued by the International Law Association in 1966, to prove its case over the Ganges; *see* Salman & Uprety, *Conflict and Cooperation*, supra note 30, at 145–146.

of Communications, Flood Control, Water Resources and Power on behalf of Bangladesh (the 1977 Agreement).[161]

The 1977 Agreement was signed almost a year after the consensus statement was adopted by the United Nations General Assembly, and about seven weeks before the start of the 1978 lean season. The consensus statement, no doubt, put pressure on both parties to reach an agreement. The political change in Delhi had certainly made the agreement easier for India, and the dawning of the lean season also must have put pressure on Bangladesh because they had witnessed the adverse effects the diversion of water had had during the previous lean season.

The agreement consisted of 15 articles, a schedule, and a side letter. It was divided into three parts: A: Arrangements for Sharing the Waters of the Ganga at Farakka; B: Long-term Arrangements; and C: Review and Duration. The preamble stated the determination of the parties to promote and strengthen their friendship and good neighborliness, and the desire of promoting the well-being of their people. It also referred to the desire of sharing, by agreement, the waters of the international rivers flowing through the territories of the two countries, and making the optimum utilization of the water resources of the region through joint efforts.

The preamble summarized the approach adopted by the agreement by mentioning both the need for an interim arrangement for sharing the waters of the Ganges as well as for a long-term solution to the problem of augmenting the flow of the Ganges. It also emphasized the desire to find a fair solution to the question before the parties 'without affecting the rights and entitlements of either country other than those covered by this Agreement, or establishing any general principles of law or precedent.' Clearly, India did not want the 1977 Agreement to tie its hands in future negotiations over any of the more than 50 rivers that it shares with Bangladesh as an upper riparian.[162]

Two principles were followed in this agreement: the quantum of water to be released by India to Bangladesh would be at Farakka, and the waters to be withdrawn by India and those to be released to Bangladesh would be in 10-day periods (with 11-day periods in the case of 31-day months). The lean season would start on January 1 and end on May 31 every year. The flow reaching Farakka was based on 75% availability of the average flow from observed data for the period 1948 to 1973. The share of each country between 1 January

161 Agreement Between the Government of the People's Republic of Bangladesh and the Government of the Republic of India on Sharing of the Ganges Waters at Farakka and on Augmenting its Flows. Dacca, 5 November 1977, UNTS: 1066, I-16210.

162 For details *see* Salman & Uprety, *Conflict and Cooperation*, supra note 30, at 177.

and 31 May, for the years 1978 to 1982, was included in the schedule to the agreement.[163]

The 1977 Agreement expired in 1982, without much progress, and in that year, India and Bangladesh signed a MoU that, to address the river management issues on an interim basis, provided for a temporary allocation of water for the 1983–1984 dry seasons.[164] This MoU also expired, and India continued to operate the Barrage in 1985 without a legal instrument.

A second MoU was signed to address Barrage operations between 1986 and 1988, which also expired. The period between 1989 and 1996 passed by without a formal legal instrument governing the sharing of the Ganges by the two countries. Finally, in 1996, India and Bangladesh signed a treaty on sharing the Ganges River at Farakka.[165] In effect today, it is set to expire in 2026.

2.1.2.1.1 Operational Rules of the 1996 Ganges Treaty

The Ganges Treaty 1996 is rather brief and the main points that are recorded are on the sharing of a part of the water. The main objective is to determine the amount of water released by India to Bangladesh at the Farakka Barrage. The Ganges Treaty relies on a formula for sharing water.[166] In the first scenario, when the River flows are 70,000 cubic feet per second (cfs) or less, each nation receives half the available flow. In the second scenario, Bangladesh has a fixed allocation of 35,000 cfs and India receives the rest (the 'balance of flow'). In the third scenario, India receives 40,000 cfs and Bangladesh receives the rest.[167]

The preamble of the Treaty stresses the desire of both countries to share and optimally utilize the water resources for flood management, irrigation, basin development and hydropower generation for mutual benefit. Guided by the principles of equity, fairness, and no harm to either party, both commit to concluding water sharing agreements regarding 54 other common rivers. Discouraging unilateral development, the Treaty also recognizes the necessity of coordinated management of the watercourses and cooperation to find a solution to the problem of augmenting the Ganges flow during the dry season. Further, Treaty specifies that the sharing arrangements will be reviewed at

---

163 *Id.*

164 *Id.*

165 *See* A. Swain, '*Reconciling Disputes and Treaties: Water Development and Management in Ganga Basin*', 6:1 Water Nepal (1998) 43–65; *see also* Salman & Uprety, *Conflict and Cooperation*, supra note 30.

166 Treaty on Sharing the Ganges Water at Farakka, India–Bangladesh, 12 December 12, 1996, 36 I.L.M. 519 (1996) (Ganges Treaty).

167 *Id.*, art. IX.

five-year intervals or earlier to make any needed adjustments. These provisions appear to endorse the principles of equitable and reasonable utilization and the no harm obligation, along with the theory of limited territorial sovereignty.[168]

2.1.2.1.1.1 *Regulatory Rules of the Ganges Treaty*

It is noteworthy that India has explicitly acknowledged, through this treaty, the Ganges as an international river, and recognized the mutual need of a solution to the long-term problem of augmenting its flow. The preamble states as follows:

> [B]eing desirous of sharing by mutual agreement the waters of the international rivers flowing through the territories of the two countries and of making the optimum utilization of the water resources of their region in the fields of flood management, irrigation, river basin development and generation of hydro-power for the mutual benefit of the peoples of the two countries.

In a similar vein, Article VIII states:

> The two Governments recognize the need to cooperate with each other in finding a solution to the long-term problem of augmenting the flows of the Ganges during the dry season.[169]

For the sharing of the water, as noted above, specific periods and amounts of water are agreed upon in the first three articles of the treaty. Furthermore, Article IX states that the principles of equity, fair play, and no harm to either party will be considered in the case of an emergency of low water level, and the necessary adjustments to the agreement will be made. The Treaty, signed for a period of thirty years, incorporates a provision for review to take place every five years.[170]

2.1.2.1.1.2 *Institutional and Dispute Resolution Rules under the Ganges Treaty*

The institutional provisions of the Treaty are set out in Articles IV to VII. One of the outcomes of the agreement substantiated by the Treaty is the constitution

---

168 *See* S. M. A. Salman, '*Sharing the Ganges Waters Between India and Bangladesh: An Analysis of the 1996 Treaty*', in S. M. A. Salman & L. Boisson de Chazournes, 'International Watercourse—Enhancing Cooperation and Managing Conflict', Technical Paper No. 414, *World Bank* (Washington, DC, 1998) 127–154.

169 *Id.*, art. VIII.

170 *Id.*, art. X.

of a Joint Committee. The Committee consists of representatives nominated by the two governments in equal numbers. Its main task, per the Treaty, is 'implementing the arrangements contained in the Treaty and examining any difficulty arising out of the implementation of the above arrangements and of the operation of Farakka Barrage.'[171] In addition, the Committee is responsible for setting up joint teams at the Farakka Barrage and Hardinge Bridge to observe and record the daily flows. These data must be submitted to both governments, alongside a yearly report. When further actions are needed because of the report, the governments shall meet to decide upon this.[172]

What is interesting is that although its preamble acknowledges both parties' wish to find a fair and just solution without affecting the rights and entitlements of either country, the Ganges Treaty does not include any elaborate dispute resolution provision. Article VII merely states that if the Joint Committee fails to resolve an implementation-related dispute, it should be referred to the Indo-Bangladesh Joint Rivers Commission (JRC).[173]

The JRC, composed of a chairman and three members each from Bangladesh and India, holds ordinary sessions four times a year and special meetings of *ad hoc* experts nominated by the parties, as needed.[174] All its meetings are in camera unless decided otherwise. While in accordance with Article 4 of the JRC Statute, its functions are limited to flood control, it also discusses the problems of, and undertakes joint investigations on, the lower part of the Ganges River, but does not have any power to allocate water. Similarly, it has no remit to settle disputes; they should be referred to the two governments,[175] which at an appropriate level resolves them by mutual discussion.[176] The parties to the Treaty, it appears, chose political/diplomatic means, not legal ones, to resolve disputes.

2.1.2.1.2 Progress Status on India—Bangladesh Shared Waters Relations

More than two-thirds of the 30 years during which the Ganges Treaty is to remain in force have elapsed. However, the two countries have failed to reach an agreement on a mechanism to augment the flow of the Ganges and to

171 *Id.*, art. VII.
172 *Id.*, art. VI.
173 *Id.*, art. VII.
174 For the details of the working of the Joint Rivers Commission, *see* Salman & Uprety, *Conflict and Cooperation*, supra note 30, at 134–135.
175 R. R. Iyer, *Water: Perspectives, Issues, Concerns* (New Delhi: SAGE Publications; Strategic Foresight Group, 2013).
176 Ganges Treaty, supra note 166, art. VII.

provide sufficient amounts of water for both parties[177] with the view of ensuring water security for each country. As discussed above, this was the crux of the matter in the dispute on the Ganges River and its Treaty negotiations. Nor have the two countries made a breakthrough on any of the other 54 rivers they share. Therefore, the main expectations of the Treaty have not been met.[178] One observer noted, 'Farakka offers a warning about how not to handle transboundary rivers to prevent complex subcontinental water sharing problems from becoming crisis in the future.'[179]

However, the Treaty has helped India and Bangladesh contain their protracted dispute revolving around the sharing of the Ganges waters.[180] It can even be argued that the relative peace resulting from the Treaty facilitated the conclusion of the Framework Agreement on Cooperation for Development by the two countries in 2011, fifteen years after conclusion of the Treaty, as discussed below.

177 *See* generally, P. J. Smith & Lt. Col. C. H. Gross, *Water and Conflict in Asia?* (Honolulu, HI: Asia-Pacific Center for Security Studies 17 September 1999).

178 By solely obliging the two parties to divide the waters, the Treaty relegated the fundamental issues of flow augmentation, flood mitigation, and basin management to formalities, and mentioned them almost as an afterthought. It is, thus, an embodiment of the failure of sovereignty-based water agreements in South Asia to enhance water security and incentivize regional cooperation. *See* M. S. Huda, '*Envisioning the Future of Cooperation on Common Rivers in South Asia: A Cooperative Security Approach by Bangladesh and India to the Tipaimukh Dam*', 42:1 Water International (2017) 54–72, at 58. If built, the Tipaimukh Dam in Manipur, India, on the Barak River downstream of the confluence of Barak and Tuvai Rivers, will generate 1,500 MW of hydropower and enhance flood control. However, it would also lead to the drying up of two main rivers, the Surma and the Kusiyara, which meet much of the irrigation needs of northeastern Bangladesh, in addition to adversely impacting the environment and bio-diversity of the lower riparian areas of Bangladesh. *See* Z. Kibria & R. Laifungbam (eds.), *Tipaimukh Hydroelectric Multipurpose Project: Dam or Damage?* (Dhaka: BanglaPraxis & CORE,2003) at 13–14. *See also* Huda, *id.*

179 C. Colopy, *Dirty, Sacred Rivers: Confronting South Asia's Water Crisis* (Oxford: Oxford University Press, 2012) (Chapter 'Beyond Barrage and Boundaries') at 305.

180 An observer noted that despite the general perception that the issue of Ganges water sharing between India and Bangladesh was resolved with the Treaty signing, many issues remain. The Treaty may be considered a stopgap measure in a persistent river water dispute. The 2026 deadline will force the stakeholders (the governments of India and Bangladesh, the West Bengal government, and all concerned political parties) to make important decisions regarding this river in a situation further aggravated by climate change and innumerable political developments that are impossible to predict. *See* P. Pandey, '*Bangladesh, India, and Fifteen Years of Peace: Future Directions of the Ganges Treaty*', 54:4 Asian Survey (July/August 2014), 651–673, at 673.

2.1.2.1.3 India–Bangladesh Framework Agreement on Cooperation for Development

On 6 September 2011, the Governments of Bangladesh and India signed, in Dhaka, the Framework Agreement on Cooperation for Development.[181] The purpose of the Framework is to record and formalize their desire to promote transborder cooperation in the management of shared water resources, hydropower potential, and ecosystems and in the areas of connectivity, and trade and economic cooperation.

The Framework Agreement states that to enhance cooperation in sharing the waters of common rivers, both parties will explore the possibility of common basin management of common rivers for mutual benefit. Further, they will cooperate in flood forecasting and control, and provide necessary assistance to each other to enhance navigability and accessibility of river routes and ports.[182]

According to one observer, Barrister Rashid, the Agreement may not have received adequate attention. It covers cooperation with India in almost all matters and ushers in a new phase of Indo-Bangladesh relations.[183] Indeed, according to Barrister Rashid, clearly, in the past, India always insisted on dealing with Bangladesh on the Ganges water issue at a bilateral level, and rejected Bangladesh's proposal in the 1970s for engaging co-riparian Nepal for the augmentation of the waters of the Ganges. By signing the Agreement, India has departed from its past stance of bilateralism (the Agreement refers to the benefits of multilateralism) and has finally agreed on cooperation at sub-regional and regional levels in areas such as water, energy, food security, and environmental degradation.[184]

The Agreement consists of 12 articles. They deal with promotion of trade, investment, and economic cooperation through progressive removal of tariff and non-tariff barriers and facilitation of trade through connectivity for bilateral and sub-regional use; water sharing of common rivers through exploring

181 Available on the Government of India, Ministry of External Affairs, website, http://www.mea.gov.in/bilateral-documents.htm?dtl/5218/Framework_Agreement_on_Cooperation_for_Development_between_India_and_Bangladesh.

182 Id., art. 2.

183 Barrister H. U. Rashid, '*Indo-Bangladesh Framework Agreement*', The Daily Star (18 July 2012). To illustrate this position, one may note the last paragraph of the preamble of the Agreement, *id.*, which states: 'Convinced that cooperation at the bilateral, sub-regional and regional levels will accelerate development and enable the two countries to realize their developmental aspirations, shared destiny and common vision of a peaceful and prosperous South Asia.'

184 *Id.*

the possibilities of their common management as a basin; technical cooperation and exchange of information with respect to natural disasters; cooperation in energy including renewable resources; promotion of scientific, cultural, educational, and people-to-people exchange; cooperation in environmental protection; sub-regional cooperation in the power sector, water resources management, and physical connectivity; cooperation on issues relating to their national interests; and cooperation in security. The Framework Agreement also reiterates that neither party shall allow the use of its territory for activities harmful to the other[185] and provides for a Joint Consultative Commission for effective implementation of the Agreement,[186] amendment of the Agreement by mutual consent, and entry into force.[187] While the Agreement is a welcome development, the devils are in the details of some of its Articles, such as Articles 2, 8 and 12. They are each discussed briefly below.

Water-sharing of some major common rivers (54 major rivers flow to Bangladesh from India) is a priority issue and 'life—blood' question for the people of Bangladesh. Sharing is to be based on the common basin management system. Under Article 2, the parties agreed only 'to explore the possibilities of common basin management of common rivers' and therefore the commitment is only to explore, and not an agreement on sharing waters of common rivers based on common basin management.

Article 2 also states that both parties will 'provide necessary assistance to each other to enhance navigability and accessibility of river routes and ports.'[188] This may arguably include the cooperation of Bangladesh to enhance the navigability of India ports (*viz* Kolkata port), and India may at some point raise with Bangladesh the insufficiency of the flow of the feeder canal of Farakka Barrage to flush the silt of Hooghly River. Furthermore, Bangladesh may have to provide India more water to the feeder canal for the Kolkata port.

Article 8 is unclear as to what the parties meant by close cooperation on 'issues of national interests' as Articles 1 to 8 cover almost all areas of cooperation. Given the geopolitical and economic realities, the 'national interests' of India may not be deemed as 'national interests' of Bangladesh and, accordingly, the Article may lead to uncertainty and misinterpretation.[189]

Article 12 on the process of termination of the Agreement envisages first that the Agreement can be terminated by mutual consent. Second, the Agreement

---

185 *Id.*, art. 9.
186 *Id.*, art. 10.
187 *Id.*, art. 11.
188 *Id.*, art. 2.
189 *See* for some discussions, Rashid, supra note 183.

can be terminated by giving written notice to the other party providing the reasons for seeking such termination. Thereafter, the parties hold consultations to address the reasons cited by the party in the Joint Consultative Commission. The Article further provides that actions taken or agreement reached pursuant to the Agreement shall not be affected by its expiry.[190] It is not clear why the termination of a bilateral agreement has been made so difficult unless a lurking suspicion exists that the agreement may not be found favorable to a party after a certain period. In many situations, the weaker party would prefer to seek termination of the agreement.[191] Furthermore, it is quite unusual to prescribe to a sovereign party to provide reasons to the other party for termination and to hold mandatory consultations with the other party on termination of a bilateral agreement. It is an inherent right of a party to terminate any bilateral, or any other, agreement by providing written notice in advance of a certain period. It is also unusual to note that 'agreements reached' without actions taken on them 'shall not be affected' by expiry or termination of the Agreement.[192] Any agreements reached can always be terminated after its expiry. Only actions already taken pursuant to agreements are not terminated.

Despite the above weaknesses, the Agreement overall opens possibilities in cooperation on bilateral, sub-regional, and regional levels in areas such as water, energy, food security, and environmental safety and is to be welcomed. If the provisions of the Agreement are implemented promptly with good faith, the outcome may be mutually beneficial.[193] It could also be argued that the provision on enhancement of cooperation has also been considered as a landmark in favor of rekindling the spirit of cooperation that existed between India and Bangladesh when the latter emerged as an independent state in 1971.[194]

On the whole, the situation regarding sharing the waters of the Ganges between India and Bangladesh, as well as any of the other fifty plus rivers, seems quite uncertain. No agreement on the augmentation of the Ganges River has been concluded and data sharing is still *ad hoc*.[195] Moreover, the Framework Agreement is awash with generalities, and no concrete action on any water issue has been taken in the last seven years since it was concluded.

190 Framework Agreement, supra note 181, art. 12.

191 *See* for some discussions, Rashid, supra note 183.

192 *Id.*

193 *Id.*

194 A. Nishat, '*A Review of the Institutional Framework for Management of Water Resources in the Ganges-Brahmaputra-Meghna System*', in G. Pangare (ed.), *Hydro Diplomacy, Sharing Water Across Borders* (New Delhi: Academic Foundation 2014) 109–116, at 110–111.

195 *See* M. Nesa, '*A Step Toward Solving the South Asian Water Crisis*', Georgetown Journal of International Affairs (25 May 2015) at 2–3.

2.1.2.2 *India–Nepal Treaty Regimes on Shared Watercourses*

As indicated above, a number of agreements have been concluded by India and Nepal on their shared rivers that are tributaries of the Ganges. Such agreements include the Kosi Agreement, the Gandak Agreement, and the Mahakali Treaty.

2.1.2.2.1 The Kosi Agreement

The Kosi River, which originates in Tibet, is the largest tributary of the Ganges. India and Nepal signed an agreement in 1954 for the development and implementation of a project involving the construction of a dam and all appurtenant work to control flooding, generate electricity, enhance irrigation, and prevent erosion.

Prepared without profound reflection on either side, and in a politically fluid environment, the 1954 Kosi Agreement[196] is characterized by the presence of many flaws, some serious, and the Agreement is considered by stakeholders as a bad deal for Nepal. Multiple elements pertaining to the design, management, sharing and allocation to ensure water security, were controversial including,

1. provisions on prior approval and notification to the Nepalese government of all actions regarding project work were unclear, and relevant definitions were missing;
2. the need for the submission of data, specimens, reports, and other results of surveys by the Indian government was not clearly articulated;
3. provisions regarding water use and power allocation were unclear and emphasized India's right to regulate the Kosi River at the dam site;
4. there was no provision regarding the *modus operandi* on communicating with the Indian government on matters of increase or decrease of power supply;
5. the provisions concerning land ownership issue were ambiguous and misleading;
6. a schedule for the establishment of civic amenities (schools, hospitals, water supply and so forth) was missing; and
7. it restricted the use of waters by Nepal not only on the Kosi (main), but also on its tributaries.

The Agreement was amended in 1966 to address the above concerns by clarifying that (i) any work or activities related to the project (approval and notification, all data, specimens, reports and other results of surveys) carried out by the Indian government would be furnished to the Nepal government;

---

196 Agreement on the Kosi Project, 25 April 1954 (revised, December 1966), in Salman & Uprety, *Conflict and Cooperation*, supra note 30, at 349.

(ii) Nepal would reserve the right to withdraw water for irrigation and other purposes from the Kosi and its tributaries; (iii) the Nepalese government would communicate with the Indian government three months prior to any increase or decrease of power supply exceeding 6,800 kW; (iv) project land would be leased by Nepal to India for 199 years; (v) civic amenities would be built for the duration of the construction phase of the Project upon approval of the Nepalese government; and (vi) Nepal's rights to withdraw, for irrigation and for any other purpose, water from the Kosi River and from the Sun-Kosi River, or within the Kosi Basin from any other tributaries of the Kosi River, were re-established. However, with regards to the latter matter, India retained the right to regulate all the balance of water supply in the Kosi at the dam site. Per the revised agreement, Nepal was entitled to up to 50% of the total electricity generated by any power house located within a 10-mile radius from the dam site built by or on behalf of India. A noteworthy element is that practically all decisions on project execution can be taken by India, a *modus operandi* criticized by the Nepalese without, however, lodging any formal complaint.[197]

The Kosi Agreement also provides for a Joint Commission. The Joint Commission is responsible for facilitating coordination between the governments on matters covered in the Agreement and for considering matters of common interest (land acquisition by Nepal for lease to India, resettlement of displaced populations, implementation of the agreement, and resolution of disputes).[198]

Despite the revision, the Kosi Agreement (terminating after 199 years from 1954) continued to be considered by many to be a bad deal for Nepal with lots of inherent risks, including unmanageable flooding.[199] The skeptics were not wrong. In August 2008, there was an unusually severe breach on the eastern embankment above the Kosi Dam. First, water flowed out and impacted the adjacent Sunsari District of Nepal. Later, the breach widened to a two-km stretch, allowing water to gush out, affecting millions in both Nepal and India.[200]

---

197 *See* Uprety, *South Asian Water Treaty Practice*, supra note 21.

198 D. Gyawali, '*Water Conflicts in Southern Riparian Lands*', in D. Gyawali (ed.), Rivers, Technology and Society. Learning the Lessons of Water Management in Nepal (London: Zed Books with Himal Books (Kathmandu), 2004) 87–118.

199 The project's barrage-building relied on engineering methods of non-silting rivers (in Europe and North America), which were inappropriate on the Kosi. *See* generally, D. Gyawali, *Poor Planning and Corruption Caused Kosi Flood*, Sci Dev Net, thttps://scidev.net/global/disasters/opinion/poor-planning-and-corruption-caused-kosi-flood.html (visited March 25, 2018).

200 The Kosi embankment collapse was not a natural disaster, but a man-made tragedy. The catastrophe resulted from an unholy marriage of 'the wrong technological choice', 'bad institutional arrangements', and 'half a century of political misconduct'. *See* Gyawali, *id.*

Against the backdrop of the havoc caused by the flood, India and Nepal decided to urgently establish a Joint River Committee at the ministerial level to discuss ways to avert such calamities in the future.[201]

2.1.2.2.2 The Gandak Agreement

The Gandaki River, also originating in Tibet, flows through central Nepal and empties into the Ganges River. In 1959, India and Nepal signed an agreement to build a dam on the Gandaki for flood control, irrigation, and power generation.[202] India paid for the dam (entirely within Nepal but close to the Indian border) as well as two large canal systems for irrigation. The Agreement contains a monthly schedule for the release of water to India for its irrigation canals,[203] and requires India to generate power and share it with Nepal.[204]

Several provisions, deemed giving sub-optimal benefits and undermining Nepal's sovereignty, became controversial. However, the most controversial provision, per experts, pertained to securing the right of Nepal to water required for irrigation or any other use inside Nepalese territory for trans-valley uses from February to April, which was curtailed by Article 9.[205] The monthly water requirements specified in the schedule to the Agreement, barring the monsoon months, were either very close to or exceeded the river flows. This provision had, thus, the effect of virtually ending all prospects for irrigation development in the Gandaki Basin within Nepalese territory.

Following protests, Article 9 was revised (on 30 April 1964). The revision removed some of the restrictions, but specified that separate agreements would be concluded for trans-valley uses of Gandaki waters from February to April. The revised Agreement may seem like an improvement, but in the absence of the separate agreement, the trans-valley uses of Gandaki waters continue to be restricted.

---

201 Minutes of the Third Meeting of Nepal India Joint Committee on Water Resources 29 September–1 October 2008), para 25.

202 Agreement between Nepal and India on the Gandak Irrigation and Power Project, 4 December 1959, available at https://www.internationalwaterlaw.org/regionaldocs/gandak-project.html. *See also* Salman & Uprety, *Conflict and Cooperation*, supra note 30, at 361.

203 Agreement, *id.* annex.

204 *Id.*, art. 8. For details about the Gandak Agreement, *see* Salman & Uprety, *Conflict and Cooperation*, supra note 30, at 83–95; A. B. Thapa, '*The Gandaki River Treaty*', 21 *Spotlight* (2002) 9–10.

205 Thapa, *id.*

Judging the adequacy of the Agreement without any data-based costs-benefits analysis of the project is an extremely difficult task. Therefore, the success of the treaty should be considered in perspective. Several shortcomings notwithstanding, at a time when international water rights were essentially based on customary law for which the importance of rivers related mainly to consumptive uses, it was laudable to have attempted to tackle issues pertaining to non-consumptive uses of water.

2.1.2.2.3 The Mahakali Treaty

The Mahakali River (called the Sarada in India), another major tributary of the Ganges, forms the border between western Nepal and India.[206] The two countries signed a treaty on 12 February 1996[207] for its overall governance (to expire after 75 years).[208] The Mahakali Treaty addresses the allocation of power from two existing barrages (the Sarada and the Tanakpur) and from a project proposed for construction (the Pancheshwar Multipurpose Project or PMP),[209] to be operated as a single project to yield 'the maximum total net benefits.'[210] The Treaty provides for a Joint Commission to collect information, facilitate information exchange, enable cooperation, and examine differences regarding treaty interpretation.[211]

It is noteworthy that the Sarada and the Tanakpur Barrages were already completed in 1920 and 1991, respectively.[212] The Mahakali Treaty simply absorbed their regimes. The only addition was the construction of the PMP and the extension of the validity period of the entire framework for another 75 years.

The Treaty endorses the principles of equitable and reasonable utilization, the equitable distribution of benefits, and an obligation not to cause significant harm. This is strengthened by a provision which, acknowledging an obligation not to cause harm, states:

---

206 Treaty Between the East India Co. (Great Britain) and the Rajah of Nepal, 2 December 1815, India-Nepal, 65 Parry 351. The treaty established the border between India and Nepal.

207 India-Nepal Treaty Concerning the Integrated Development of the Mahakali River, 12 February 1996, 36 I.L.M. 531 (1997) (Mahakali Treaty); *see also* Salman & Uprety, *Conflict and Cooperation*, supra note 30, at 373.

208 Mahakali Treaty, *id.*, art. 12.

209 For background on treaty negotiations, *see* T. Upreti, *International Watercourses Law and Its Application in South Asia* (Kathmandu: Pairavi 2006) at 180–256.

210 Mahakali Treaty, supra note 207, art. 3.

211 *Id.*, art. 9.

212 *See* Upreti, supra note 209.

> In order to maintain the flow and level of the waters of the Mahakali River, each Party undertakes not to use or obstruct or divert the waters of the Mahakali River adversely affecting its natural flow and level except by an agreement between the parties.[213]

The use of the waters by the local communities living on both sides of the Mahakali, not exceeding 5% of the average annual flow at Pancheshwar, is excluded from the purview of the undertaking,[214] but the parties' obligations to maintain the natural flow of the River is clear.

The Treaty further acknowledges the right of parties to independently develop and operate any work on the tributaries of the Mahakali as long as it does not affect the rights of the other.[215] However, any project to be developed on the Mahakali where it forms the boundary should be designed and implemented under an agreement based on the principles established by the Treaty.[216] Hence, there is an obligation for both countries to reach an agreement before commencing any project on the Mahakali.[217] The two parties can also plan joint undertakings.[218] While restricting unilateral development of the River, the Treaty further obligates the parties to abide by its principles (equality, benefit sharing, and no harm) and endorses the principles of cooperation and information sharing.[219] Interestingly, the term 'no harm' is not defined, thus any interpretation will need to rely on the definition provided by general international water law.

The Treaty further states that the PMP shall be designed to produce the maximum total net benefit. All benefits accruing to the parties (power, irrigation, flood control) shall be assessed, and the costs shall be borne in proportion to the benefits accrued. As important, the Treaty emphasizes the notion of

---

213 Mahakali Treaty, supra note 207, art. 7 (italics added).

214 *Id.*

215 *Id.*, art. 8.

216 *Id.*, art. 6.

217 This *lex specialis* goes beyond the requirements of *Lake Lanoux Case* (France v. Spain) in which Spain had claimed that given the existence of the Treaty of Bayonne and the Additional Act, both of 26 May 1866, certain works that France was undertaking that required the utilization of the waters of Lake Lanoux could not be undertaken without a specific agreement between the parties. However, the tribunal ruled that in carrying out such works, France was not committing a breach of the provisions of said Treaty and the Additional Act. For discussion, *see* S. McCaffrey, *The Law of International Watercourses: Non-Navigational Uses* (Oxford: Oxford University Press, 2001) at 197–203.

218 S. M. A. Salman & K. Uprety, '*Hydro-politics in South Asia: A Comparative Analysis of the Mahakali and Ganges Treaties*', 39 Natural Resources Journal (1999) 295–339.

219 Mahakali Treaty, supra note 207, preamble and art. 9.

sharing of benefits from water uses rather than the sharing of water, and the reference to notions of 'maximum benefit', 'benefit sharing', or 'mutual benefit' are used in acknowledging the principle of equitable utilization.[220]

The Treaty provides for a Mahakali River Commission, to be guided by the principles of equality, mutual benefit, and no harm to either party. Composed of equal numbers of representatives and with expenses shared equally, its functions pertain to inspecting all structures covered by the Treaty, making implementation recommendations, evaluating, monitoring and coordinating plans of action, and examining differences concerning its application.[221] If the Commission is unable to resolve a dispute, a three-member arbitral tribunal will be formed. Both Nepal and India will nominate one arbitrator, with neither nominating its own national, and the third arbitrator will be appointed jointly to preside over the tribunal. If the parties are unable to agree on the third arbitrator within 90 days, either country may request the Secretary-General of the Permanent Court of Arbitration (PCA) to appoint an arbitrator. The reference of the PCA certainly gives credence to the dispute-resolution mechanism, which is further strengthened by another stipulation that the decision of the tribunal is final and binding.[222]

2.1.2.3 *Partial Observations*

Despite the multiple problems in interpretation due to lack of clarity, the treaties concluded for managing the Ganges system need to be recognized as having served a good purpose. They not only created an environment for countries to discuss and attempt to manage international waters within a legal framework as civilized nations, but also created a possibility for further enhancement of the cooperative aspects of the treaties.

Creative approaches may have been tried, but the outcomes have not proven to be optimal.[223] These creative approaches may have brought the issues of

---

220 *See* generally, *id.*, art. 3.

221 *Id.*, art. 9.

222 *Id.*, art. 11.

223 To circumvent the stringent constitutional requirement in Nepal, which calls for at the highest level of political scrutiny, a variety of project-specific private-public contracts for sharing of benefits from the Karnali, the Seti, or the Arun Rivers, for instance, have been engineered by successive governments. Not surprisingly they have been criticized by most stakeholders. *See also* above Section 2.1.2.2 of this monograph; see also generally, Gautam, B., & A. Shah, '*Law Ministry Opposes West Seti Renewal, Advises Against New Clauses*', Republica (November 2009); Johnson, L., '*Advocacy Strategies for Promoting Greater Consideration of Climate Change and Human Rights in Development Activities: The Case of the West Seti Hydroelectric Project in Nepal*', 27: 2 Pace Environmental Law Review (2010); Shrestha, R. S., "Opinion," *West Seti Project. A Nepali Perspective* (September 2008);

international water management within juridical purview, but have generated, in many instances, confusion and ambiguities.

2.2 *Regimes for Shared Watercourses under Discussion*

2.2.1 The Teesta River Dynamics

The Teesta River, shared by India and Bangladesh, originates from Cholamo Lake at an elevation of 17,487 feet a.s.l in the Indian Himalayas. Fed by several rivulets rising in the Thangu, Yumthang and Donkia-La ranges, the River then flows southeast and meets its main tributary, the Rangeet River, and at which point it changes course southwards, flowing entirely into West Bengal. The River hits the plains at Sevoke, where it is spanned by the Coronation Bridge, which links the northeast Indian states to the rest of India. The River then courses its way to Bangladesh, before finally merging with the Brahmaputra.[224]

2.2.1.1 *The Teesta River Regime*

The history of sporadic negotiations between India and Bangladesh (formerly East Pakistan) on the Teesta can be traced back to the 1950s, although these were relatively slow-paced and without outcomes.[225] After the emergence of independent Bangladesh, the Joint Rivers Commission (JRC) became more proactive. While meeting on a variety of issues related to the Teesta, among others, the JRC recognized that sharing its waters needed to be based on scientific studies that were to be completed by the Joint Teesta Committee by the end of 1985. Pending completion of such studies, in the spirit of friendship and good neighborliness, and for purposes of regulating temporary water provisioning to both counties, an *ad hoc* arrangement for sharing of the Teesta flows during the dry season was concluded on 20 July 1983, to be valid until the end of 1985. This *ad hoc* arrangement was not formally signed but was attached to the minutes of the JRC.[226] It allocated 36% of the waters of the Teesta for Bangladesh, 39% for India, and left the remaining 25% unallocated for maintaining the flows. The parties further agreed that the secretaries in charge of irrigation in both governments would, based on the *ad hoc* arrangements, prepare a formal document spelling out the locations for sharing, the modality for

---

Uprety, K., '*Nepal's West Seti Project Imbroglio: The Supreme Court Speaks*', 2 Beijing Law Review (2011) 17–24.

224 Encyclopedia Britannica (adapted). *See also* M. F. Islam, '*The Teesta River and Its Basin Area*' (Chapter 2), in *Water Use and Poverty Reduction* (Springer, 2016) at 13.

225 S. Prasai & M. D. Surie, *Political Economy Analysis of the Teesta River Basin* (New Delhi: The Asia Foundation, 2013).

226 Salman & Uprety, *Conflict and Cooperation*, supra note 30.

flow measurement, and the technicalities for monitoring the implementation, and would present their recommendations for consideration by the JRC within 90 days.[227]

In 2004, an India–Bangladesh Joint Technical Team produced the first draft agreement on the Teesta.[228] However, in a meeting held in Delhi the same year, Bangladesh, in consideration of its long-term water security concerns, raised fresh issues, making a major shift from its earlier stances on the 1983 *ad hoc* arrangement. It proposed that 10% of the Teesta waters be kept for natural flow, 39% for India, 36% for Bangladesh, with the remainder distributed proportionately between the three. India, on the other hand, insisted on the completion of scientific studies first. Finally, with reciprocal compromises, both sides agreed and planned to seal the agreement on the use of the Teesta River in 2011, but the signing was delayed because of failure to reach a consensus on the uses of Brahmaputra River.[229]

In 2011, Delhi and Dhaka finalized another interim arrangement for 15 years, under which India would get 42.5% and Bangladesh, 37.5% of the Teesta's waters during the dry season. The deal also included the setting up of a joint hydrological observation station to gather accurate data for the future.[230] However, due to opposition in West Bengal, the arrangement was shelved when it was due to be signed. While delays continue, the Teesta is drying up, following construction of several barrages in both countries, negatively impacting the free flow on its 414-km journey to the sea.[231]

2.2.1.2 *Problems and Parleys in India–Bangladesh Water Relations*

The failure to reach an agreement on the sharing of the waters of the Teesta between India and Bangladesh is a classic example of how the periphery can influence the center in the process of foreign policy-making in India.[232] The Union government could not reach an agreement with a foreign state due to the objections raised by the Chief Minister of a state government. A similar trend is also evident in India's foreign policy towards its neighbors, where the

227 Uprety, *South Asian Water Treaty Practice*, supra note 21.
228 Prasai & Surie, supra note 225.
229 Uprety, *South Asian Water Treaty Practice*, supra note 21.
230 M. Mirchandani, '*The Teesta Water Dispute: Geopolitics, Myth and Economics*', ORF Special Report No. 25, Observer Research Foundation (New Delhi, 21 September 2016).
231 Significant barrages include the Farakka Barrage in Bangladesh, the Teesta Barrage at Gojoldoba in West Bengal, and the two hydroelectric dams in Sikkim.
232 Kadurugamuwa, supra note 19, at 69.

Indian states sharing land or maritime boundaries with neighboring nation states have a tangible influence on the Center in policy-making.[233]

The Teesta River dispute cannot be taken only as an isolated phenomenon as it is intricately connected to other important bilateral issues. For example, India is faced with the problem of accessing its landlocked northeastern states as Bangladesh does not allow overland transit to India through its territory. The transportation of goods to these states and vice versa is being done with much difficulty through the circuitous Siliguri Corridor. Bangladesh will not strike a deal allowing India overland access to its northeastern states until India agrees to share the waters of the Teesta.[234]

The Teesta River problem is not likely be resolved until the West Bengal government exhibits a certain degree of flexibility, as was done by the former Chief Minister Jyoti Basu in the case of the Ganges Treaty. The Teesta issue is still contentious and influences the foreign policy behavior of India and Bangladesh in relation to each other. In May 2012, for instance, during a visit to India, Bangladesh Foreign Minister Dr. Dipu Moni warned that the bilateral relations would be complicated if India failed to deliver on the Teesta water sharing agreement. Ironically, just one day before Dr. Moni made her remarks, Indian External Affairs Minister S. M. Krishna had issued assurances that India was committed to an early resolution of the Teesta water issue. Therefore, the Bangladesh Foreign Minister's statement could well be attributed to the doubts among the Bangladeshi polity about India's good faith in negotiating and implementing bilateral water sharing agreements.[235]

2.2.2 The Brahmaputra Basin Dynamics

The earliest legal instrument affecting the Brahmaputra, a major international river shared by China, India, Bhutan, and Bangladesh, is the 1914 Shimla Convention[236] through which Great Britain, Tibet, and China fixed the boundaries between India and Tibet. This resulted in the 'McMahon Line' from Bhutan to the Great Bend (the area where the Brahmaputra River emerges from its Tibetan course into the Assam Valley of India), which substantially moved the border north, making India one of the riparians of the Brahmaputra Basin.[237]

233 An example would be the Indian State of Tamil Nadu influencing the central government in its behavior towards Sri Lanka.

234 Kadurugamuwa, supra note 19, at 69.

235 *Id.*

236 Convention Between Great Britain, China, and Tibet, 3 July 1914, *see.* http://www.tibetjustice.org/materials/treaties/treaties16.html.

237 G. Ping & M. D. Shwan, *Brahmaputra River*, Max Planck Encyclopedia of Public International Law, Max Planck Institute for Comparative Public Law and International Law, Heidelberg, and Oxford University Press London (August 2007).

However, despite these agreements, the Brahmaputra, even now, lacks a multilateral or basin-wide water sharing framework.[238] The arrangements that exist are bilateral, narrow in scope, and more importantly, fragmented.

2.2.2.1 *China–India Water Relations*

In 1954, China and India signed a MoU for sharing Brahmaputra hydrological data for flood protection purposes,[239] which, however, ended with the 1962 Sino-Indian War.[240] Then, after a long pause, starting in 2002, they concluded a series of MoUs pertaining to the River: the 2002 MoU on the Provision of Hydrological Information of Brahmaputra River in Flood Season by China to India and its Implementation Plan[241] (expired in 2007);[242] the 2008 MoU on the same topic[243] and its Implementation Plan for the 2008–2012 period; and the 2013 MoU on the same topic, which is currently in effect.[244]

The 2013 MoU deals with flood control and disaster mitigation in the downstream regions of the Brahmaputra River and focuses on the provision by China of hydrological information to India. Article 1 lays down its foundation, namely friendly cooperation, mutual benefit, good faith and equality, elements that are repeated in several of China's transboundary water agreements. Wouters and Chen consider these principles to be in accord with the country's approach in this field, with a focus on peaceful diplomacy (the duty to cooperate and equitable and reasonable utilization).[245] It must be emphasized that the scope of 2002 MoU was limited to flood control and hydrological information. The 2008 MoU had expanded the scope to information sharing regarding data use

238 *See* Y. Liu, '*Transboundary Water Cooperation on the Yarlung Zangbo/Brahmaputra: A Legal Analysis of Riparian State Practice*', 40:2 Water International (2015) 354–374.

239 *See* A. Roul, '*India-China Hydro Diplomacy: Beyond Information Sharing MOUs*', Society for the Study of Peace and Conflict (22 March 2013), http://www.sspconline.org/opinion/IndiaChinaHydroDiplomacy_22032013. The text of the MOU is unavailable.

240 *See* Roul, *id.*

241 *See* Liu, supra note 238.

242 Cited in '*China to Offer Hydrological Data to India*', People's Daily (25 April 2002), http://www.china.org.cn/english/MATERIAL/31573.htm.

243 Memorandum of Understanding (MoU) on Provision of Hydrological Information of the Brahmaputra Yaluzangbu River in Flood Season by China and India (2008), http://wrmin.nic.in/forms/list.aspx?lid=349.

244 Memorandum of Understanding (MoU) on Provision of Hydrological Information of the Brahmaputra Yaluzangbu River in Flood Season by China and India, 23 October 2013, http://mea.gov.in/bilateral-documents.htm?dtl/22368; *See also* Liu, supra note 238; P. Wouters, '*International Law: Facilitating Transboundary Water Cooperation*', TEC Background Papers No. 17, Global Water Partnership (Stockholm, 2013) at 17.

245 P. Wouters & H. Chen, '*China's "Soft-path" to Transboundary Water Cooperation Examined in the Light of Two UN Global Water Conventions: Exploring the "Chinese Way"*', 22 Journal of Water Law (2013) 229–247.

in flood forecasting and mitigation. But under Articles 5 and 6 of the 2013 MoU, China agrees to provide documents on the state of the Brahmaputra's catchment area as well as historical information regarding floods, natural disasters and any abnormal rise and fall of water levels or discharges that might lead to sudden flooding.

Under Article 10 of the 2013 Implementation Plan, India agreed to financially compensate China for data provision.[246] Recall that the duty to share data and to compensate for such data are notable international law principles directly deriving from the UN Watercourses Convention,[247] which professor McCaffrey considers is within the realm of 'distributive justice.'[248]

On specific technicalities of cooperation, Article 2 identifies three Chinese stations for the provision of hydrological information (Nugesha, Yangcun, and Nuxia), and Article 3 specifies that the information will pertain to water level, discharge, and rainfall and is to be provided daily from 1 June to 15 October. The Indian Central Water Commission and the Chinese Bureau of Hydrology and Water Resources are the official implementing agencies of the Sino-Indian MoU. An Expert-Level Mechanism established in 2006 pursuant to a Joint Declaration by the two countries (also referred to in Article 11 of the Implementation Plan attached to the 2013 MoU) is responsible for interacting and cooperating on the flood-season hydrological data, emergency management, and other trans-border river issues.[249]

In parallel to the above, China and India also signed, in 2013, an MoU for the strengthening of cooperation on all Sino-Indian transboundary rivers.[250] This

---

246 S. Ho, '*River Politics: China's Policies in the Mekong and the Brahmaputra in Comparative Perspective*', 23:85 Journal of Contemporary China (2014) 1–20.

247 United Nations Convention on the Law of Non-Navigational Uses of International Watercourses, 21 May 1997, art. 9 (Regular Exchange of Data and Information).

248 *See* S. C. McCaffrey, '*The Codification of Universal Norms: A Means to Promote Cooperation and Equity*', in L. Boisson de Chazournes et al. (eds.), *International Law and Freshwater: The Multiple Challenges* (Cheltenham: Edward Elgar, 2013) 125–139, at 135.

249 The 2013 MoU does not include any provisions on dispute settlement; perhaps they were deemed unnecessary because of its narrow scope. The 2008 MoU on the Provision of Hydrological Information between China and Bangladesh (infra note 259), and the 2002 MoU on the Provision of Hydrological Information of the Upper Stream of Zuo River during Flood Season between Vietnam and China also are devoid of dispute settlement provisions. China appears to favor the principle of peaceful settlement of disputes, as illustrated by its water agreements with Kazakhstan, Mongolia, and Russia. This also means that it is inclined to address disputes through consultations or negotiation. See Wouters and Chen, supra note 245.

250 Memorandum of Understanding between the Ministry of Water Resources, the Republic of India and the Ministry of Water Resources, the People's Republic of China on Strengthening Cooperation on Trans-border Rivers, 23 October 2013. The text of the MoU

MoU for cooperation touches upon the legal issues of scope, substantive as well as procedural rules, institutional mechanisms and dispute settlement to varying degrees. On the matter of scope, it is important to note that the use of the term 'trans-border rivers' is quite specific, limiting the legal reach to only rivers, thus excluding other bodies of water. Nonetheless, the scope is broad enough to cover the natural resources and environment of all riparian countries. Both countries recognize transboundary rivers as well as their related natural resources and environment and connect them with socio-economic development, and implicitly display a wish to sustainably utilize them. This broadness (Article 1), in addition to being inclusive, opens the door for an integrated water resources management approach.

On substance, with only five provisions, the MoU for cooperation is quite limited in scope and largely reaffirms past cooperation. Articles 2 and 5 refer to the Expert Level Mechanism, and the provision of flood-season hydrological data, emergency management, and the exchange of views on issues of mutual interest. Article 3 reiterates India's appreciation for China's provisioning of hydrological information, and Article 4 extends the Brahmaputra River data sharing period.[251]

Regular exchange of data and information, notes Christina Leb, is a duty closely linked with the effectiveness of cooperation on transboundary water systems and information is essential for the administration and sustainable development of rivers.[252] Leb further notes that the UN Watercourses Convention considers this duty a general principle because it acknowledges its importance for successful cooperation on effective management of transboundary waters.[253] Equally important, exchange of data regarding the Brahmaputra becomes a highly relevant issue in that a major diversion dam on its Yarlung Tsangpo section (Zangmu Dam), which became operational in 2015 and was built allegedly without prior knowledge of the downstream riparians, is now considered a threat by them due to its alleged significant adverse consequences downstream.[254]

---

is reproduced on the Government of India, Ministry of External Affairs website, http://www.mea.gov.in/bilateral-documents.htm?53/Bilateral/Multilateral_Documents.

251 *Id.*, arts. 3 & 4.

252 C. Leb, *Cooperation in the Law of Transboundary Water Resources* (Cambridge: Cambridge University Press, 2013) at 115.

253 *See* generally *id.*, at 115.

254 '*China's Great Dam a Threat to Millions in India*', Probe International, reproducing Daily Bhaskar (24 June 2011); *see also* A. Sasi, '*As Clearances Turn into Hurdles, Brahmaputra Edge Lost to China*', Indian Express (21 October 2015).

However, it seems that such exchange of data and information has been subject recently to the ups and downs of the overall political and diplomatic climate and relationship between India and China. It was reported in October 2017 that since May 2017,

> China has declined to share hydrological data with India on the Brahmaputra River ... Beijing is now withholding key data from Delhi during flood season, exerting pressure after a feud between India and China over a disputed Himalayan region.[255]

Beijing blames out-of-date hydrological stations for the lack of data.[256] Thus, the territorial disputes between India and China[257] have clearly overshadowed the attempts towards cooperation on their shared watercourses.[258]

2.2.2.2 *China–Bhutan–Bangladesh Water Relations*

China has not yet formalized diplomatic relations with Bhutan due to unresolved border issues between the two states. Regarding Bangladesh, on the other hand, in 2008, China concluded an MoU to supply hydrological information during the flood season.[259] In March 2015, another MoU was signed on the sharing of rainfall data in the River's catchment area in China, which was

---

255 Environmental experts estimate that the Brahmaputra River's total water flow will fall roughly 60% due to the dam. *See* Ankurvaidya, '*Water Wars with Specific Reference to Asia*', SCRIBD (undated), https://www.scribd.com/document/82796138/Water-Wars-With-Specific-Reference-to-Asia.

256 *See* T. John, '*How China Could Weaponize Water*', Time Magazine (3 October 2017) at 8, http://time.com/4951207/how-china-could-weaponize-water/. The report further indicated that '[e]xperts fear that China could divert the river's waters away from India, devastating its Northeastern plains. A water treaty might prevent that scenario, but Beijing may not be inclined to relinquish control of the faucet.'

257 India and China have territorial disputes along the border of Arunachal Pradesh, including a 25,900 km^2 area in the regions of Snag, Demchok, and Aksai. Similarly, India and Bangladesh have disputes over the alluvial land as it changes course. India and Nepal have a territorial dispute along the Kalapani River. Kashmir is the bone of contention between India and Pakistan.

258 One author has noted that in the South Asia region, territorial and water disputes are interrelated and need particular attention. Moreover, the water conflict is the major problem that influences the remaining regional issues. *See* Z. Hassan, '*Way Forward to South Asian Water Crisis*', 01:01 Journal of South Asian Studies (2013) 35–49, at 46.

259 Memorandum of Understanding upon Provision of Hydrological Information of the Brahmaputra Yalunzangbu River in Flood Season by China to Bangladesh (on file with the authors).

aimed at helping Bangladesh forecast floods.[260] So far these are the only legal instruments pertaining to Sino-Bangladesh cooperation on the Brahmaputra River, and primarily target flood control.

2.2.2.3 *Bhutan–India Waters Relations*

The Bhutan–India political relationship started in 1949 with the signing of a Treaty of Friendship, which exchanges Indian non-interference in the internal administration of Bhutan for Bhutanese agreement to secure India's advice on foreign relations.[261] Since its origin, the Treaty, which was updated in 2007,[262] has been the basis for present-day joint hydropower cooperation on Brahmaputra tributaries in Bhutan to export electricity to India.[263]

2.2.2.3.1 Jaldhaka, Chukha and other Agreements between India and Bhutan

The economic cooperation, more precisely, began on 23 September 1961 with the signing of the Jaldhaka Agreement between India and Bhutan,[264] which enabled construction of the barrage in the Bhutanese territory and 27 MW power plant in West Bengal, India with a provision for (i) royalty payment, (ii) 250 kW free power from the project for Bhutan (or 1.314 GWh free annual energy), and (iii) import of power (to Sibsoo, Chamurchi and Phuntsholing) to Bhutan from India.[265]

---

260 *See* N. Samaranayake et al., *Water Resource Competition in the Brahmaputra River Basin* (Arlington, VA: CNA, 2016) at 32, 84.

261 Treaty of Friendship Between India and Bhutan, 8 August 1949, art. 2.

262 The updated version used more malleable language and stated that both governments shall cooperate closely with each other on issues relating to their national interests and that neither government shall allow the use of its territory for activities harmful to the national security and interest of the other (Article 2). A report notes that the revised treaty recognizes Bhutan's and India's 'sovereignty and territorial integrity', which previous treaties did not. From an Indian perspective, as noted by the report, Bhutan offered a stable political system and a positive investment environment. While it has recently transitioned from a monarchy to democracy, Bhutan has remained stable, certainly in contrast to India's other neighbors. G. Price & S. Mittra, *Water, Ecosystems and Energy in South Asia Making Cross-Border Collaboration Work*, Chatham House Research Paper (London: Royal Institute of International Affairs, June 2016) at 41.

263 The main tributaries of the Brahmaputra River in Bhutan are the Drangme (Manas), the Puna Tsang (Sankosh), the Wang (Raidak), and the Amo Rivers.

264 The Jaldhaka River is a 192 km transboundary river that originates from the Kupup or Bitang Lake in southeastern Sikkim and flows through Bhutan and West Bengal (India). After that point, the River enters Bangladesh through the Lalmonirhat district and then joins with the Dharla River until it debouches into the Brahmaputra River. Due to the River's wandering over several international borders, only a small length of the River lies within Bangladesh.

265 '*Bhutan's Isolation to End*', Economic and Political Weekly (Mumbai) (23 September 1963).

The Jaldhaka Project was followed by the Chukha Hydro-Electric Project (CHEP).[266] Under the 1974 Agreement on the CHEP, which laid the foundation for inter-basin transboundary cooperation and benefits-sharing between the two countries,[267] India provides financial resources for the project (Article 3) and Bhutan sells all the surplus electricity (approximately 70%) generated by it to India (Article 8).[268] With several other agreements signed subsequently,[269] some scholars regard the hydropower cooperation between Bhutan and India as a model for how transboundary water bodies can be jointly managed by basin-sharing countries to promote regional economic development.[270]

2.2.2.3.2 Particularities of India–Bhutan Agreements

The governments of India and Bhutan have customarily reiterated that the key undertone to their relationship is mutual benefit.[271] The norms and spirit deriving from the friendship arrangements are translated into cooperation agreements for each respective project. However, the feasibility studies, detailed project reports, environmental impact assessment, strategic impact assessment, resettlement and rehabilitation plans, compliance monitoring reports, and other such documents are not made publicly available, obstructing genuine appraisal of already implemented projects.[272] However, superficial, subjective, and informal surveys of projects make it possible to assess the scope and form of relations between those implemented with assistance from India and those implemented with assistance from others. Based on such surveys, some noticeable patterns can be identified.

2.2.2.3.3 Noticeable Patterns in India–Bhutan Water Relations

While the agreements are not in the public domain, many Bhutanese share concerns (albeit informally) that the level of control of each country in implementation of projects is skewed in favor of India, with major and strategic

266 '*Bhutan Rivers Watch*', International Rivers, (16 June 2015), https://www.internationalrivers.org/resources/9059.

267 S. Shrestha et al., *Managing Water Resources Under Climate Uncertainty* (Springer, 2015).

268 N. P. Banskota, *South Asia Trade and Energy Security: The Role of India* (Boca Raton, FL: Universal-Publishers, 2012), http://www.bookpump.com/upb/pdf-b/2331742b.pdf.

269 For details, *see* Lamballe, supra note 26, at 58–60. *See also Bhutan Rivers Watch*, supra note 266.

270 A. K. Biswas, '*Cooperation or Conflict in Transboundary Water Management: Case Study of South Asia*', 56:4 Hydrological Sciences Journal (2011) 662–670.

271 Vasudha Foundation, *A Study of the India-Bhutan Energy Cooperation Agreements and the Implementation of Hydropower Projects in Bhutan* (New Delhi, 2016) at 24.AN.

272 *Id.*

decisions vested with appointees of India.[273] However, the collaborative and seemingly friendly nature of the relationship between Bhutan and India with regard to transboundary water resource management, according to one scholar, can be attributed more to Bhutan's far-sightedness and political adeptness than to India's attempts at creating more equitable regional relations.[274] Bhutan has been able to manage transboundary water interactions in a way that creates positive sum outcomes.[275]

2.2.3 Partial Observations

As the above discussion and analysis show, treaty-making on shared water resources in South Asia has always been a challenging task, particularly due to lack of data, lack of trust, and absence of political will. When data is scarce and willingness to cooperate is lacking, achieving quick results becomes difficult. And when all sides are not of equal political strength, do not give equal importance to the issues of concern, or have different perspectives, the pace for finalization and conclusion of treaties can be slow and intermittent.

2.3 *Riparians' Perspectives on Water and Benefit Sharing*

Based on location, interests, political strength, and preparedness, the perspectives of the riparian countries in South Asia *vis-à-vis* their national water security are strikingly different and contrasting. Bangladesh, for instance, insists that the Ganges and Brahmaputra are two separate river basins, and that they should be managed independently without any inter-basin water transfer. Accordingly, the augmentation of the Ganges water should be resolved within the Ganges Basin through storage reservoirs in Nepal, which Nepal is against and considers impractical as well as unconscionable. On the other hand, India insists that diverting water from the Brahmaputra is the optimal solution for flow augmentation, and for resolving water problems in both the Ganges and Brahmaputra Basins. There is also an unresolved dilemma between the proposals of Bangladesh and India, whether to share water over time or space.[276] The problems that the Farakka Barrage in the Ganges River caused highlight

---

273 *See* for some discussion, *id.*, at 24.

274 P. Hanasz, '*Power Flows: Hydro-Hegemony and Water Conflicts in South Asia*', 10:3 Security Challenges (2014) 95–112, at 108, https://www.regionalsecurity.org.au/Resources/Files/SC10-3%20Hanasz.pdf.

275 *Id.*, at 109.

276 *See* B. Crow et al., *Sharing the Ganges: The Politics and Technology of River Development.* (New Delhi: Sage Publications, 1995).

the concerns by Bangladesh that India has similar plans to siphon off water from the Brahmaputra River, as well as the Meghna River.[277]

India prefers to divert water from the Brahmaputra Basin to the Ganges Basin to increase agricultural production. In India, arable land in the Ganges Basin (600,000 km^2) is considerably larger than that of the Brahmaputra Basin (55,000 km^2). India is striving to develop the enormous hydropower potential in the Brahmaputra Basin to meet the increasing energy demand of the country. It promotes Brahmaputra water resources and hydropower development through bilateral cooperation with Bhutan, excluding China and Bangladesh.[278]

Bhutan, given the history of friendly cooperation with India, has achieved economic and social development through the export of hydropower to India.[279] Thus, for Bhutan, exploiting hydropower potential with financial and technical support from India is a prime concern.

China, with a preference for internalization, wants to utilize the huge hydropower potential of the Brahmaputra to meet its growing energy demand and to divert water from this basin to other water scarce river basins in that country. China, like India, has also chosen a unilateral approach to the Brahmaputra Basin's hydropower and water resources development that excludes India and Bangladesh.[280]

As indicated by one study, the upper riparians (China and India) are more concerned about the Brahmaputra Basin in political terms, whereas the lowest riparian Bangladesh is primarily concerned about the Basin in physical terms.[281] These perceptional differences rarely facilitate the conclusion of treaties, and the solutions become even more remote when countries have not ratified or acceded to any international legal framework. Thus, each riparian's perspective (as in many other regions) adds another challenge to the sharing and managing of water resources in the South Asia region.

---

277 M. M. Rahman & O. Varis, '*Integrated Water Management of the Brahmaputra Basin: Perspectives and Hope for Regional Development*', 33:1 Natural Resources Forum (February 2009) 60–75, at 73–74; see also Rahman, M. M., '*Hydropower Ambitions of South Asian Nations and China: Ganges and Brahmaputra Rivers Basins*', 4:1/2 International Journal of Sustainable Society (2012) 131–157.

278 *Id.*

279 Biswas, supra note 270.

280 Rahman & Varis, supra note 277.

281 *See* Samaranayake et al., supra note 260, at iii (executive summary).

Part 3: South Asia and the United Nations Watercourses Convention

The competing demands, concerns for achieving and enhancing water security at national level, intra-regional power imbalances, and absence of an inclusive legal regime have complicated the South Asian countries' sharing of transboundary waters and sustaining the common goal of balancing the riparian ecosystems. Although the 1997 UN Convention on the Law of the Non-navigational Uses of International Watercourses (UNWC) is widely believed to have codified the basic customary international water law principles,[282] none of the South Asia countries has joined the Convention.[283] India and Pakistan abstained from the vote at the General Assembly, while Afghanistan and Bhutan were absent. Bangladesh and Nepal voted in favor of the Convention,[284] but neither has ratified or acceded to the instrument.[285] Also, China, an 'upstream superpower',[286] and 'a most enthusiastic champion' for the principle of sovereignty,[287] voted against the Convention,[288] a move characterized

282 *See* Salman, *Entry into Force of the UN Watercourses Convention*, supra note 10.

283 All South Asian countries are members of the UN. However, Bhutan and Nepal have not accepted the compulsory jurisdiction of the ICJ, while India and Pakistan accept it with reservation. China, which had shunned participation in international adjudications for decades, has shifted its position and now accepts limited jurisdiction of the ICJ. Only Bangladesh accepts the jurisdiction of the ICJ *in toto*. For an excellent discussion regarding China, see J. Ku, '*China and the Future of International Adjudication*', 27 Maryland Journal of International Law (2012) 154–173.

284 See K. Uprety, '*Specially Invited Opinions and Research Report of the International Water Law Project: Global Perspectives on the Entry into Force of the UN Watercourses Convention 2014: Part One*', Gabriel Eckstein (ed.), 16 Water Policy (2014) 1198–1217.

285 An author has flagged that Nepal's vote in favor of the Convention was cast, in New York, by mistake, without any consultation with the Nepalese capital. *See* Lamballe, supra note 26, at 17.

286 E. J. Nickum, '*The Upstream Superpower: China's International Rivers*', in O. Varis et al. (eds.), *Management of Transboundary Rivers and Lakes* (Berlin and Heidelberg: Springer, 2008) 227–244.

287 T. Wang, '*International Law in China: Historical and Contemporary Perspectives*', 221 Recueil des Cours: Collected Courses of The Hague Academy of International Law (1990) 195–369.

288 Delegate Gao Feng of China during discussions on the UN Watercourses Convention noted that there were obvious drawbacks in the draft convention. First, it failed to reflect general agreement among all countries, and several states had major reservations regarding its main provisions. Secondly, the text did not reflect the principle of the territorial sovereignty of a watercourse state. Such a state had indisputable sovereignty over a watercourse that flowed through its territory. There was also an imbalance between the rights and obligations of the upstream and downstream states. He further said China could not support provisions on the mandatory settlement of disputes, which went against the principles set out in the United Nations Charter. His government favored the settlement of all disputes through peaceful negotiations. Accordingly, he would vote against the draft

as a significant reassertion of its absolute territorial sovereignty approach.[289] China has avoided multilateral diplomacy as a way to solve shared water challenges.[290] It has centered its diplomatic outreach on the Brahmaputra issue at a bilateral level.[291] In addition, it has been reluctant to participate in multilateral water agreements, even at a regional level.[292] This varying and confused response of the countries of South Asia to the UN Watercourses Convention is indicative of the attitude towards international water law discussed above, including mistrust and misunderstanding of the provisions of the Convention.[293]

---

resolution to which the draft convention was attached. *See UNGA Press Release GA/9248* (21 May 1997). Burundi and Turkey are the only two other countries to join China in voting against the Convention.

289 D. Seligman, *World's Major Rivers: An Introduction to International Water Law with Case Studies* (Las Vegas: Colorado River Commission of Nevada, 2008), http://crc.nv.Gov/docs/Worlds_Major_Rivers.pdf. Some authors, however, have also noted that international water law has actually influenced China, as there are similarities between the 1997 UN Watercourses Convention and China's Water Law of 2002. *See* J. D. Fry and A. Chong, '*International Water Law and China's Management of Its International Rivers*', 39 Boston College International & Comparative Law Review (2016) 226–266, at 226; *see also* P. Wouters, '*Commentary, Considering China's Approach to the UN Watercourses Convention: Time to Revisit?*', International Water Law Project, https://www.internationalwaterlaw.org/blog/2014/07/28/professor-patricia-wouters-considering-chinas-approach-to-the-un-watercourses-convention-time-to-revisit/ (suggesting that China's transboundary water resources management must be considered within a broader context, and as part of a continuum of China's evolving approach to international law). Although China voted against the UNWC, it answered the UNWC's call by signing two agreements on transboundary waters with Kazakhstan and Russia in 2001 and 2008 respectively. All the agreements and chapters generally include the principles set out in the UNWC.

290 J. Wuthnow, '*Water Power, Water Worries: China's Goals and Challenges as the Brahmaputra's Uppermost Riparian*', in N. Samaranayake et al., *Water Resource Competition in the Brahmaputra River Basin: China, India and Bangladesh* (Arlington, VA: CNA, May 2016) at 34.

291 *Id.*, at 33.

292 *Id.*, at 34. This can be noticed in China's approach *vis-à-vis* the Mekong River Commission, established in 1995. Although China has been a dialogue partner, it has refused to seek full membership, largely due to the concern that doing so would impose restrictions on its upstream dam building plans. *See id.*, citing Ho, River Politics (2014) (see note 247) at 34. Myanmar is also a dialogue partner in the Commission.

293 For a thorough discussion of the misunderstandings about the Convention, *see* S. M. A. Salman, '*The United Nations Watercourses Convention Ten Years Later: Why Has its Entry into Force Proven Difficult?*', 32:1 Water International (2007) 1–15.

3.1 *South Asia's General Malaise about International Water Law*

An all-encompassing conclusion about the discomfort of the countries of South Asia *vis-à-vis* the UN Watercourses Convention is difficult due to their diversified interests and perceptions, and power asymmetry. Nevertheless, informal surveys of scholars suggest that the discomfort is due essentially to the perceived inability of the Convention to tackle all the possible region-specific problems, and the differing needs and demands among the countries. Two main reasons influenced by historical, political and cultural elements come into play.

First, these countries consider the principles of water use emanating from the Convention, though intuitively appealing, difficult to operationalize and implement in the heated geopolitical environment of South Asia. The many principles contained therein and designed to ensure cooperation in the abstract, are considered vague and, in view of some, even contradictory.[294] They are deemed unsuitable for resolving South Asia-specific issues where the prevailing language is centered on the idea of water as a national security priority and on which there are contrasting views amongst stakeholders and opinion builders.[295] Such concerns are prevalent among some technocrats in South Asia, notwithstanding the high hopes built on the entering into force of the UN Watercourses Convention in August 2014.[296]

Moreover, there are those who, relying on a realist analysis, see water scarcity and riparian rights to water allocations as part and parcel of state security. Countries where this analysis dominates appear reluctant to engage in multilateral agreements over water because these agreements inherently require the secession of some portion of their national sovereignty, and its approach to the concept of water security.[297] Also, there are those historical materialists who endorse multilateral water sharing cooperation but believe that such cooperation can only be based on an 'unfair' allocation of water skewed towards more developed (or bigger) states. Countries where this analysis

---

294 *See id.*

295 The stakeholder related problems and the dilemma of developing a sound resources policy is well depicted in the context of Nepal in a publication by Ratan Bhandari, *Jholama Khola* (River in the Pocket) (Nepal Federation of Water and Energy Consumers, 2012).

296 *See* Salman, *Entry into Force of the UN Watercourses Convention*, supra note 10.

297 On adequately managing sovereignty over water issues, *see* generally Green Cross International, *National Sovereignty and International Watercourses* (Geneva: Green Cross International, 2000) at 8, http://www.greencrossitalia.it/ita/acqua/wfp/pdf/international_watercourses_2000.pdf.

dominates remain unclear, and perhaps confused, as to the contents as well as the methodology for negotiating water agreements.[298]

Second, the treaty-making behavior in South Asia, particularly concerning transboundary waters, is quite unique.[299] Due to their prevailing mutual distrust, inability to delink hydropower from water resources, lack of clarity on their real minimal needs to ensure their perceived national water security, and reservations about generalizing policy to avoid establishing a precedent, the strategic approach of some countries is merely to theoretically engage in water-related initiatives, but practically to advance only those initiatives that serve their specific interests.[300] An interesting twist can further be noted in the case of India. Being in a unique geographic position (upper riparian *vis-à-vis* Pakistan and Bangladesh, and lower riparian *vis-à-vis* Nepal and China), India employs a differentiated strategy and, thus, considers a uniform formula for the management of water relations to be impractical and unadvisable.

3.2 *Countries' Specific Concerns over the UN Watercourses Convention*

Individual South Asian countries have their own stance concerning the provisions of the UN Watercourses Convention, which goes beyond the realm of water security. For instance, Pakistan considers that 'groundwater' should not be part of the definition of a 'watercourse' (Article 2) because it is difficult to determine the geographic range of aquifers hydraulically linked to rivers and that it is inequitable to include aquifers located entirely within the territory of one country.[301] India takes the stance that Article 3 of the Convention, which

298 *See* generally B. G. Verghese & R. R. Iyer (eds.,), *Harnessing the Eastern Himalayan Rivers: Regional Cooperation in South Asia* (New Delhi: Konark Publishers, 1993) at 274; *see also* Uprety, *Specially Invited Opinions*, supra note 284.

299 Lacking a regional governance framework for transboundary water management and limiting water relations to only a few bilateral water-sharing treaties having vague clauses and redressal mechanisms are specific to South Asia, as we have seen throughout this monograph.

300 Many agreements, with ambitious proposals to develop an array of projects are concluded, but the further design and implementation of such projects are deliberately delayed. In this type of situation, particularly prevalent in Nepal, the countries' right to develop projects on their own is practically foreclosed.

301 Ahmad Kamal, delegate of Pakistan, said he had participated in the work on the draft convention. However, despite the Working Group's efforts, not all concerns had been adequately reflected. Pakistan had reservations regarding draft Articles 2, 7 and 33. In draft Article 2, there were difficulties in using the term 'groundwater'. While the flow of a river could be measured in precise terms at various gauging sites, it was not possible to do so with groundwater, which flowed slowly through porous soil. Different laws applied to the flow of rivers and ground-waters. With respect to draft Article 7, he said its use of the term 'significant' before 'harm' was problematic in that significant could be subject to

ensures a nation's right to enter into watercourse agreements, contradicts its domestic law whereby water is constitutionally a state rather than a Union matter.[302] It also claims that the term 'sustainable', as used in Articles 3 and 5 in the context of 'sustainable utilization', is not properly defined. In addition, all the countries in the region seem to employ different interpretations of the word 'significant' in the context of 'no significant harm' (Article 7). Some of the countries oppose the provision on equality of access to transboundary remedies (Article 32), which they interpret as presupposing regional integration.[303] While Pakistan is displeased that the dispute settlement provision (Article 33) is not binding, India is dissatisfied that the provision contains elements for mandatory third-party intervention.[304]

With respect to China, it had also participated in the process of negotiation and drafting of the UNWC, but decided at the end to vote against the Convention. However, despite this negative vote, China has borrowed from and adopted some of the basic principles of the Convention in its own transboundary waters agreements. Its reservations about the UNWC concern a number of articles, as discussed above. Experts on China's transboundary water governance issues give several reasons for its reservations.

First, generally, the contents the UNWC are too detailed to be easily understood, digested, and accepted. China's transboundary water treaties use comparatively simple rules and language. Second, the UNWC pays more attention to the interests of downstream countries than those of upstream countries, an objection raised by some upstream countries. For example, they see the obligation not to cause significant harm, the notification on planned measures, and the functions of the fact-finding Commission impose heavier obligations on upstream countries. Being an upstream country, China does not agree with several of these rules.[305] Moreover, until recently, China considered international water law as prescribing that only upstream riparians can harm downstream riparians by affecting the quantity or quality of water

different definitions. He favored obligatory and binding settlement procedures. Pakistan had reservations regarding draft article 33 on dispute settlements because the mechanism provided therein was not binding. *See UNGA Press Release GA/9248* (21 May 1997). *See also* Salman, *UNWC Ten Years Later*, supra note 293.

302 *See* in this connection, Section 2.1.1.7 of this monograph 'Effects of the Indus Waters Treaty on National Water Governance.'

303 Uprety, *Specially Invited Opinions*, supra note 284.

304 While admitting that it is not uncommon, Professor McCaffrey has noted surprise in the reservations of these countries given the mild form of dispute resolution methods under the Convention. *See* S. McCaffrey, '*Watercourses Convention: The Convention Enters into Force*', 44:4 Environmental Policy and Law (2014), 351–356 at 351.

305 Uprety, *Specially Invited Opinions*, supra note 284.

flow to them. In fact, this erroneous view has been corrected. It is now widely acknowledged that downstream riparians can also harm upstream riparians by foreclosing their future uses of water through the prior use of and the claiming of rights to such water.[306]

Third, in the dispute settlement mechanisms, submission to arbitration and referral to the ICJ are seen as quite strict. China has never accepted the jurisdiction of the ICJ and cannot accept the current mechanism of dispute settlement as long as the methods of dispute resolution are mandatory. The authority of the fact-finding Commission is too broad (it has access to the respective territories and the power to inspect any facility, plant, equipment, construction, or natural features), which could damage state confidentiality or commercial secrets. These extensive powers are also an infringement on state sovereignty, which China values very highly.[307]

A fourth concern relates to domestic procedural requirements, which are complex and lengthy. If China were to decide to join the Convention, it could only join by accession, because Article 34 of UNWC provides that 'the Convention shall be open for signature by all states and by regional economic integration organizations from 21 May 1997 until 20 May 2000.' The time for signature had therefore elapsed. If China decides to accede to the Convention, China's Law on the Procedure of the Conclusion of Treaties would apply.[308] Per Article 7.2 of the Procedural Law, the UNWC is a multilateral treaty 'relating to territory and delimitation of boundary lines.' Per Article 11, which details the procedure of accession to multilateral treaties or agreements, the Ministry of Foreign Affairs, or the relevant department under the State Council together with the Ministry of Foreign Affairs, must review the treaty and then make recommendations to the State Council for approval. The State Council must then submit its recommendations to the Standing Committee of the National People's Congress for final decision to accede. The instrument of accession is then signed by the Minister of Foreign Affairs. Treaties that China accedes to

306 For a detailed analysis of this matter, *see* S. M. A. Salman, *'Downstream Riparians Can also Harm Upstream Riparians: The Concept of Foreclosure of Future Uses'*, 35 Water International (2010) 350–364 at 350. The article has been translated to and published in Mandarin. *See* S. M. A. Salman, *'Downstream Riparians Can also Harm Upstream Riparians'*, (Chinese version) translated by D. Hu and Z. Tang, in G. Tan and L. Kong (eds.), *Symposium Proceedings for International Law and Practice of Transboundary Water Resources* (Beijing: China Social Sciences Academic Press, March 2012) 38–62.

307 *See* Chen, supra note 23.

308 *See id.*

are not subject to ratification.[309] Such lengthy and complex procedures, and the fact that China has been one of three countries that voted against the Convention, may stand in the way of China acceding to the Convention. Thus, the fact that none of the countries of the South Asia region is a member of the UNWC may remain in effect for some time to come.

Part 4: Conclusion: 'Cooperation'—South Asia's Missing Pillar

The contemporary characteristics of the continent of Asia, in general, as pointed out by many scholars, are quite varied.[310] The same observation would be accurate about South Asia region in specific. The variety is significant in that (i) the region is relatively state-centered, and traditional norms of state sovereignty and domination remain primordial; (ii) not all countries are equal in influence, because of their asymmetry in economic or political terms; (ii) countries are marked by strategic uncertainty; (iv) some of the countries possess increased economic capacity for military modernization, thus leading to a security dilemma; (v) there is a proliferation of informal frameworks designed and proposed by non-governmental groups; and (vii) systemic change represented by the ending of the Cold War has reduced the intensity of ideological division.[311] These characteristics, in a collective manner, no less influence these countries' approach and position regarding their national water security concerns.

When thinking of geopolitics as a method of foreign policy analysis that seeks to understand, explain, and predict international political behavior, more specifically, the above characteristics, indeed, play a major role. As such, the countries of South Asia also have been influenced historically by these characteristics in their hydro-political behavior; such influence being more evident after the independence of India, and the emergence of two new states, Pakistan and Bangladesh. Their hydro-political behavior has been influenced predominantly by the variation in access to the waters of transboundary rivers, which is caused by topographical discrepancies and the geographical variables

309 *See* Chen, supra note 23; *see also* generally, Chen et al., supra note 23.

310 *See* generally, S. M. Pekkanen et al. (eds.), *The Oxford Handbook of the International Relations of Asia* (Oxford: OUP, 2014), Chapter 1, at 4–8.

311 *Id.* One should caution that these characteristics are not uniquely and exclusively relevant for South Asia, but these elements, the authors emphasize, are more obvious in South Asia and impact that region more intensely.

of river flow. One manifestation of this political behavior is, thus, the increased emphasis on water security and the resultant weak water management systems. This emphasis has also led to a subsequent manifestation, namely, the generalized lack of political trust among the countries in South Asia and the absence of cooperation over shared watercourses. Those issues, in turn, complicate hydro-relations and impede dispute resolution amongst them, in particular on the issue of sharing.

Water security issues transpire in multiple forms and shapes, oftentimes as a subset of issues, and complicate bilateral relations. As discussed in this monograph, Bangladesh—India relations have been strained by the diversion of the Ganges River, the Tipaimukh Dam (under planning), the proposed Indian inter-linking of rivers project, and the Teesta water-sharing predicament, in addition to India's plans to construct several dams in Sikkim (on the Teesta). Interestingly, while the Ganges Waters Treaty also purports to manage the dry season flow of the River and to seek ways to augment flows at the Farakka Barrage (Indian side) and Hardinge Bridge (Bangladesh side), research has shown that dry season flow significantly declined at the Hardinge Bridge after the commissioning of the Farakka Barrage. This severely hurts Bangladesh and has led many in Bangladesh to regard the specific purpose of the treaty to be meaningless. Moreover, because the two countries do not have a common database regarding the Ganges River and because data dissemination is not systematic, key aspects of their dispute remain unresolved, fueling political suspicion.

Water disputes between India and Bangladesh, for instance, have been subsumed under the overall difficult relations that have persisted between the two nations since the birth of Bangladesh. As would be expected, they see the disputes from different vantage points. Bangladesh views the Ganges dispute as triggered by the 'unilateral diversion' of the waters of the Ganges by India at the Farakka Barrage, which was detrimental to Bangladesh's water security concerns. Consequently, it considers that the resulting reductions in flows had severe adverse effects on Bangladesh, and the situation reflects a classic case of a more powerful country not fully concerned about the legitimate interests of a smaller and weaker neighbor. This view is prevalent throughout Bangladesh, and it regularly becomes a significant issue in the nation's electoral politics.

Bangladesh continues to raise concerns, primarily attributable to perceptions that the quantity of water received does not match expectations brought about by the Ganges Water Treaty. At face value, tensions between Bangladesh and India may appear to be sparked by conflict over water, but as noted in a report,

> it is not always a case of conflicts over water resources leading to a worsening of political relations, though that does happen on occasion; it is more often a case of a difficult political relationship rendering the water issue more intractable.[312]

Bangladesh had pleaded with India for a 'minimum guarantee' agreement (regarding the water flow), which led the two countries to conclude the 1996 Ganges Treaty. But many political parties in both countries were dissatisfied with the treaty, and several Indian states, including Bihar and Uttar Pradesh, complained that their interests had not been properly considered.

India, however, which is satisfied with the outcome of the Ganges Treaty, subscribes to a different view. The perception within the Indian bureaucracy is that Bangladesh is extremely rigid and unreasonable regarding this issue, and has greatly over-stated its water needs. The problem is, no doubt, also rooted in India's federal structure, and the fact that water in India is a state responsibility. Indeed, individual Indian states tend to view the Indian central government as overly generous toward Bangladesh, at their expense. As a result, from a political perspective, the water dispute between India and Bangladesh has contributed to a deterioration of relations between the two nations.

Bilateral disputes are not limited to Bangladesh and India. To some extent, the construction of the Zangmu Dam by China on the Brahmaputra River has raised concerns in India and Bangladesh, and multiple issues between India and Nepal on the tributaries of the Ganges are still unresolved. Over and above the disputes on water sharing, territorial disputes complicate the scene in the South Asia region. Disputed borders are both the cause and symptom of tension amongst neighbors, exacerbating the trust deficit.

Data sharing on international watercourses, as noted above, is another common problem among the countries of South Asia. One of the reasons is that water has been overwhelmingly expounded as being in the arena of 'national security', which results in considerable emphasis on water security. This has led each country to hold firm to its hydrological data, resulting in the failure to exchange even basic information about transboundary rivers. Such information includes, by necessity, stream and sediment flow and water withdrawal use data. Securitization has also led to complexities when multiple power centers control water, and where states/provinces, rather than the central governments, have legal authority over water resources.

312 *See* generally, R. R. Iyer, '*Ganga Waters: Dispute and Resolution*', paper prepared for the "Water and Conflict in Asia Seminar" held at the Asia-Pacific Center for Security Studies, Honolulu, Hawaii (17 September 1999); on file with authors.

What is important is that, in these countries, water is treated as a zero-sum resource. This makes it nearly impossible to do anything on the transboundary front before resolving the domestic national security issues. For instance, in India, the states of Haryana, Punjab, and Rajasthan have an ongoing dispute over the sharing of the waters of the Ravi, Beas, and Sutlej Rivers. In Pakistan, Punjab and Sindh provinces have an ongoing dispute over the sharing of the Indus waters under the 1991 Indus System Waters Apportionment Accord. Complexities also intensify due to the absence of provisions in most water treaties in South Asia on emerging challenges such as the impact of climate change, variable rainfall patterns, and water sharing in the light of falling groundwater levels. This is ironic in a region where floods have been a serious issue.

While some countries in South Asia appear to genuinely favor a multi-country approach, historically, collective multilateral attention to the problems of transboundary waters has been rare, and along with conspiracy theories and blame games, bilateralism prevails and triumphs, albeit slowly, with tremendous hesitance and caution. Water has differing but clear impacts on regional relations, and water disputes exacerbate already strained bilateral relations. Bangladesh and Nepal consider the Indian approach to water as a primary source of distrust. Afghanistan blames Pakistan (and Iran) for its water problems, while Nepal, Bangladesh and Pakistan blame India for theirs. Within India and Pakistan, the actions of upstream provinces/states are blamed for water shortages downstream. This blame culture, reflecting the absence of trust that plagues intra-regional relationships, makes multi-country river-sharing arrangements and cooperation daunting tasks that are particularly difficult to materialize.

In the South Asia region, initiating discussions for treaties is difficult because of legal tradition. While China's adherence to 'limited territorial sovereignty' has influenced its state practice, India, as a mid-stream riparian nation state, vacillates between absolute territorial integrity and absolute territorial sovereignty in support of its stance, depending on its location on the respective shared watercourse. Similarly, if Nepal, an upstream country, has always embraced the territorial sovereignty approach, downstream Bangladesh appears to moderate its position and adopts a limited territorial sovereignty approach, like Bhutan, which does so through its bilateral agreements with India on hydropower projects. Although attempts to establish regimes for the selected segments in the Ganges-Brahmaputra-Meghna Basin have been made, their smooth functioning has proven to be difficult, and contentious issues transcending countries remain unresolved, perhaps because of the variety in approaches.

Finally, treaty-making in the region has always been a challenging task, because of lack of data, trust, and political will. Consequently, when data is scarce and willingness to cooperate is lacking, achieving results becomes difficult. More importantly, when all sides are not of equal political strength or do not give equal importance to the issue of concern, the pace for negotiating and finalizing a treaty can be slow.

In the past two decades, the issues of cross-border water utilization, management, and mega-irrigation or hydroelectric projects affecting the riparians have gradually taken center-stage in defining interstate relations. However, issues such as upper versus lower riparians, prior use, quantum of share versus country needs, generalized mistrust, countries' physical limitations and political apprehensions blur the debate and have delayed decision-making. Given the depleting water resource, the problems of security, distribution, and management are bound to be exacerbated[313] and to invite not only countries but also provinces to engage in more conflicts since a general inclusive framework agreement to settle such conflicts is missing.

The difficulties and problems discussed above should not hide some positive messages—the silver lining—that can also be depicted from these treaty relations. Overall, except for a few problems and contentions, the Indus Waters Treaty remains a success story. Indeed, as noted above, '[w]hen a treaty is negotiated over ten years and is approved and signed at the highest level, it must be presumed that it was the best outcome that was possible under the given circumstances.'[314] However, one should hasten to add that these problems and contentions have been addressed and dealt with through the Treaty itself. In addition to successfully halting a bitter dispute by dividing the rivers of the Basin, the Treaty has survived continual regional hostility, including two wars between India and Pakistan. Implementing the regime has certainly been a difficult exercise, but thanks largely to the Treaty's built-in mechanisms, the parties have been able to maintain their overall spirit of cooperation and to manage their differences and disputes, despite the frequent upheavals in their

313 *See* generally, M. W. Rosegrant et al., *World Water and Food to 2005: Dealing with Scarcity* (Washington, DC: International Food Policy Research Institute, 2002), https://reliefweb.int/sites/reliefweb.int/files/resources/1B0BBA6D1080C010C1256C6E002E1D17-ifpri-water2025-16oct.pdf; for managing variability of flow, see generally Drieschova, A. et al., '*Governance Mechanisms to Address Flow Variability in Water Treaties*', 18:2 Global Environmental Change (2008) 285–295; see also Zafar, A. & R. G. Wirsing (eds.), '*Imagining Industan: Overcoming Water Insecurity in the Indus Basin*' (Springer, 2017); also Wirsing, R. G., & C. Jasparro, '*River Rivalry: Water Disputes, Resource Insecurity and Diplomatic Deadlock in South Asia*', 9 Water Policy (2007) 231–251.

314 *See* Iyer, supra note 312.

bilateral relations. Resort to the Neutral Expert in the Baglihar difference and to the court of arbitration in the Kishenganga dispute, and the outcome in both cases, should indeed be acknowledged as a major point of strength of the Indus Waters Treaty.

Regarding the Ganges system, the main observation would be that despite the multiple problems in interpretation due to lack of clarity, the different treaties concluded for managing the Ganges system have served some good purposes. They not only created a possibility for countries to discuss and attempt the management of international waters within a legal framework as civilized nations, but also created a possibility for further enhancement of the cooperative aspects of the treaties. Furthermore, they facilitated discussion on other basins, as well as on issues beyond water resources.

While the turbulent history and competing demands over the international waters of the countries of South Asia and the consequent calls for national water security have often forced them to fall into disputes, these demands have also compelled the riparians, in certain cases and instances, to cooperate. Such cooperation has been affected through modalities covering the quantitative and qualitative aspects of the waters, programs for shared resource development, and exchange of data. This, however, is not to suggest that the transboundary water relations show a pattern that is consistent amongst the riparians themselves, and with international law. Arguing that a sufficiently uniform state practice does not exist to justify their assumptions, the countries of South Asia do not accept, *in toto*, the existence of rules or principles of general international law relating to the use of international waters, a behavior also largely illustrated by their non-uniform treaty practice and reflected in their stance *vis-à-vis* the UN Watercourses Convention.

If the agreements between India and Bangladesh have mainly focused on water sharing, those between India and Nepal have attempted to address water security issues in an integrated manner by dealing with flood control, irrigation, sharing, and hydropower generation in the same composite instrument. If most treaties have taken a single river approach in sharing water, a treaty with a broader approach has divided the rivers in one basin. Similarly, if allocation has been a major problem, regime management has been a serious challenge, especially due to sovereignty concerns and deeply-rooted mistrust. Such sovereignty concerns and mistrust have caused the countries of South Asia to adopt defensive postures, including for water security, which has proven to impede cooperation by refusing to recognize other riparian needs and rights.

It is clear that the countries of South Asia need to draw common and basic understandings that are essential to resolving the many pending issues with regards to their shared watercourses and the persistent calls for water security. In so doing, these countries need to consider the highly contextual and dynamic governance systems of water; the variance of individual importance, scope, procedures, and forms of management from country to country; and the unique characteristics of each shared watercourse. They will need to devise pragmatic strategies to cater to the competing demands of their countries, provinces, and people. Such strategies should learn, adopt, and adapt from other countries, regions, and watercourses. Moreover, they need to be creative, and willing to cooperate in good faith in the exchange of data on their shared watercourses. Given the prevailing mistrust and hesitation amongst riparians to negotiate new agreements, one creative approach would be for countries and stakeholders to focus more on 'soft' power, the value of which has proven to be useful in many complex situations.[315]

Water has been called the oil of the twenty-first century.[316] The access, demand, use, sharing and management of international water have become extremely complex due to the crossing of multiple boundaries, that is, political, social, and jurisdictional, as well as physical, ecological, and biogeochemical. A study focusing on the problems of allocation of transboundary water among competing riparians with conflicting needs has concluded that the complexity in transboundary water allocation lies in the dynamic consequences of competition that arise from the interconnections and feedback among actors, processes, and institutions operating in knowledge and political

315 *See* for instance, generally, M. Zeitoun et al., '*Transboundary Water Interaction II: The Influence of 'Soft' Power*' 11:2 International Environmental Agreements: Politics, Law and Economics (2011) 159–278. The authors analyze transboundary water interaction by examining and interpreting the influence of 'soft' power therein. The 'soft' power of persuasion is understood to be exercised through discursive, and to a lesser extent, ideational means, and is interpreted in terms of compliance related to distributive (conflictual) or integrative (consensual) ends. Their focus is on inter-state water conflicts in hegemonic political contexts, where, it is found, the 'first among equals' has a greater ability to exploit soft power and to determine the outcome. Soft power is also seen to influence the choices states make or avoid in their transboundary water interaction, which explains in part how treaties intending to manage a conflict may in fact delay or perpetuate it. For example, soft power can be used by the basin hegemon to frame inequitable forms of cooperation in a cooperative light, such that unfair and ultimately unsustainable transboundary arrangements are replicated by the international donor community. Non-hegemonic riparian states also employ their capacity of soft power, though they may find themselves with little choice other than to comply with the arrangement established by the basin hegemon.

316 A. Swain, '*South Asian Regional Council* (*SARC*) *and South Asian Rivers: A Study in Water Conflict*', in M. Chatterji & B. M. Jain (eds.), *Conflict and Peace in South Asia* (*Contributions to Conflict Management, Peace Economics and Development*) (Bingley, UK: Emerald Group, 2008) 269–283.

communities.[317] Consequently, many transboundary water allocation issues have become contingent upon the dynamic changes that occur within knowledge and political communities, as well as the interactions and feedback occurring between them. In addition to understanding and addressing the contingent contextual factors that span knowledge and political communities, resolving complex transboundary water problems also needs to be guided by contextual application of two global principles—equity and sustainability—as anchors to accommodate the values and interests of the stakeholders involved in the problem.[318]

In the past couple of decades, an approach favoring integrated development for enhanced multilateral transboundary water cooperation has gained worldwide prominence. Therefore, even though bilateralism still prevails in South Asia's hydro-diplomacy, these countries will have to come up with mechanisms to make water a resource for joint and shared benefits, as can be observed in some other river basins.[319] They need to start a multilateral basin-wide approach for water and benefit sharing, along the lines of better models in other countries and continents, based on genuine cooperation and collective action.[320] Indeed, learning from other countries' experience is very

---

317 Choudhury & Islam, supra note 130.

318 Choudhury & Islam, *id.*, (abstract).

319 In Asia, the signatories to the Mekong Agreement 1995 reaffirmed the 'Mekong Spirit' that was in existence for four decades, along with concepts of international water law, mainly, the principle of reasonable and equitable utilization, obligation not to cause significant harm, principles of notification and negotiations, and duty to cooperate. The Mekong Agreement represents, per an author, a type of 'constitutional contract' for an international governance system that specifies areas of responsibility, general principles, decision-making procedures, eligibility, and organizational structure. *See* G. E. Radosevich, '*The Mekong River Agreement: Lessons Learned*', in *Shared Water Systems and Transboundary Issues (With Special Emphasis on the Iberian Peninsula): Proceedings of the Conference held at Luso-American Development Foundation, Lisbon, Portugal, March 11 and 12, 1999* (Luso-American Foundation, 2000) 333–368. Nevertheless, the fact that the Mekong Agreement is not inclusive of all six riparians should be noted. China and Myanmar are still only 'dialogue partners', not parties, to the Mekong Agreement. Thus, the Mekong Spirit—close cooperative and collective action—is confined to only four out of the six Mekong riparian countries.

320 The experience of the riparian states of the Senegal River, namely Guinea, Mali, Mauritania, and Senegal, stands out as an excellent example for an approach of benefit sharing as opposed to water sharing. Two existing dams on the Senegal River (Manaantali and Maka-Diama) are owned, operated, and their benefits shared by these four countries under several joint agreements. *See* for some discussion on the technical aspects of the dams, A. DeGeorges and B. K. Reilly, '*Dams and Large-Scale Irrigation on the Senegal River: Impacts on Man and the Environment*', Human Development Report Office Occasional Paper 2006/38, United Nations Development Programme (2006). Similarly,

important in South Asia given its large growing population, its limited water resources, the spatial and temporal variations of water resources, the large number of shared watercourses, and the challenges posed by climate change.

As discernible from the discussions throughout this monograph, the challenges of negotiating and enforcing water related treaties are enormous and multivariate. It is, therefore, only through a spirit of genuine cooperation over their shared water resources, rather than through water security sloganeering and inefficient and uncoordinated unilateral development plans, that the countries of South Asia can improve their treaty regimes, both in theory and practice, and pull their huge and increasing population out of poverty, thirst, hunger, and darkness.

Bibliography

Abbas, B. M., *The Ganges Water Dispute* (New Delhi: University Press Ltd., 1982).

Akhtar, S., '*Quest for Re-Interpreting the Indus Waters Treaty: Pakistan's Dilemma*', Margalla Papers, Special Edition, Vol. XV, No. 1, National Defence University (2011) 15–46, http://www.ndu.edu.pk/issra/issra_pub/articles/margalla-paper/Margalla-Papers-SE-2011/02-Quest-for-Re-interpreting.pdf.

Ali, C. M., *The Emergence of Pakistan* (New York: Columbia University Press, 1967).

Ankurvaidya, '*Water Wars with Specific Reference to Asia*' SCRIBD (undated), https://www.scribd.com/document/82796138/Water-Wars-With-Specific-Reference-to-Asia.

Banskota, N. P., *South Asia Trade and Energy Security: The Role of India*. (Boca Raton, FL: Universal-Publishers, 2012), http://www.bookpump.com/upb/pdf-b/2331742b.pdf.

Baxter, R. R., '*The Indus Basin*', in A. H. Garretson et al. (eds.), *The Law of International Drainage Basins* (Dobbs Ferry, NY: Oceana Publications, 1967).

Bhandari, R., *Jholama Khola* (River in the Pocket) (Nepal Federation of Water and Energy Consumers, 2012).

'*Bhutan's Isolation to End*', Economic and Political Weekly (Mumbai) (23 September 1963).

Biswas, A. K., '*Cooperation or Conflict in Transboundary Water Management: Case Study of South Asia*', 56:4 Hydrological Sciences Journal (2011) 662–670.

the Itaipu dam project, financed and jointly owned by Brazil and Paraguay, is another shining example for benefit sharing. *See* for a short introduction, '*The Itaipu Hydroelectric Dam Project, Brazil*', Power Technology (undated), http://www.power-technology.com/projects/itaipu-hydroelectric/.

Biswas, A. K., '*Indus Waters Treaty: The Negotiating Process*', 17:4 Water International (1992) 201–209.

Bourne, C., '*The International Law Association's Contribution to International Water Resources Law*', 36 Natural Resources Journal (1996) 155–216.

Briscoe, J., & U. Qamar, '*Pakistan's Water Economy: Running Dry*', Country Water Resources Assistance Strategy Report 44375, World Bank (2006).

Chellaney, B., '*From Arms Racing to "Dam Racing" in Asia, How to Contain the Geopolitical Risks of the Dam-Building Competition*,' Paper Series, Transatlantic Academy (May 2012), http://www.transatlanticacademy.org/publications/arms-racing-dam-racing-asia-how-contain-geopolitical-risks-dam-building-competition.

Chellaney, B., *Water: Asia's New Battleground* (Washington, DC: Georgetown University Press, 2011).

Chen, H., '*The 1997 UNWC and China's Treaty Practice on Transboundary Waters*', http://www.unwatercoursesconvention.org/images/2012/10/China-and-UNWC-Study.doc.

Chen, H. et al., '*Exploring China's Transboundary Water Treaty Practice Through the Prism of the UN Watercourses Convention*', 38:2 Water International (2013) 217–230.

Choudhury, E., & S. Islam, '*Nature of Transboundary Water Conflicts: Issues of Complexity and the Enabling Conditions for Negotiated Cooperation*', 155:1 Journal of Contemporary Water Research & Education (July 2015) 43–52.

Colopy, C., *Dirty, Sacred Rivers: Confronting South Asia's Water Crisis* (Oxford: Oxford University Press, 2012).

Condon, E. et al., *Resource Disputes in South Asia: Water Scarcity and the Potential for Interstate Conflict*, Report Prepared for the Office of South Asia Analysis, U.S. Central Intelligence Agency, Workshop in International Public Affairs, 1 June 2009 (University of Madison, Wisconsin, 2009).

Crow, B. et al., *Sharing the Ganges: The Politics and Technology of River Development* (New Delhi: Sage Publications, 1995).

Desai, B., & B. K. Sidhu, '*The Kishenganga Final Award: Is the Indus Waters Treaty at the Crossroads?*', 49 Political and Economic Weekly (15 February 2014).

DeGeorges, A., & B. K. Reilly, '*Dams and Large-Scale Irrigation on the Senegal River: Impacts on Man and the Environment*', Human Development Report Office Occasional Paper 2006/38, United Nations Development Programme (2006).

Drieschova, A. et al., '*Governance Mechanisms to Address Flow Variability in Water Treaties*', 18:2 Global Environmental Change (2008) 285–295.

Fry, J. D. & A. Chong, '*International Water Law and China's Management of Its International Rivers*', 39 Boston College International & Comparative Law Review (2016) 226–266.

Gandhi, G., '*Hydro-Wisdom Must Back Hydro-Diplomacy*', in G. Pangare (ed.), *Hydro Diplomacy. Sharing Water Across Borders* (New Delhi: Academic Foundation, 2014) 9–16.

Gautam, B., & A. Shah, '*Law Ministry Opposes West Seti Renewal, Advises Against New Clauses*', Republica (November 2009).

Government of India, Ministry of External Affairs, *India-Pakistan Joint Statement on Tulbul Navigation/Wullar Barrage Project*, 28 March 2012.

Green Cross International, *National Sovereignty and International Watercourses* (Geneva: Green Cross International, 2000), http://www.greencrossitalia.it/ita/acqua/wfp/pdf/international_watercourses_2000.pdf.

Gulhati, N. D. *Indus Waters Treaty: An Exercise in International Mediation* (New Delhi: Allied Publishers, 1973).

Gyawali, D., *Poor Planning and Corruption Caused Kosi Flood*, Sci Dev Net, https://scidev.net/global/disasters/opinion/poor-planning-and-corruption-caused-kosi-flood.html (visited March 25, 2018).

Gyawali, D., '*Water Conflicts in Southern Riparian Lands*', in D. Gyawali (ed.), *Rivers, Technology and Society: Learning the Lessons of Water Management in Nepal* (London: Zed Books with Himal Books (Kathmandu), 2004) 87–118.

Hanasz, P., '*Power Flows: Hydro-Hegemony and Water Conflicts in South Asia*', 10:3 Security Challenges (2014) 95–112, https://www.regionalsecurity.org.au/Resources/Files/SC10-3%20Hanasz.pdf.

Hassan, Z., '*Way Forward to South Asian Water Crisis*', 01:01 Journal of South Asian Studies (2013) 35–49.

Hearns, G., '*The Helmand River and the Afghan-Iranian Treaty 1973*', International Water Law Project Blog (23 July 2015), https://www.internationalwaterlaw.org/blog/2015/07/23/the-helmand-river-and-the-afghan-iranian-treaty-of-1973/.

Ho, S., '*River Politics: China's Policies in the Mekong and the Brahmaputra in Comparative Perspective*', 23:85 Journal of Contemporary China (2014) 1–20.

Huda, M. S., '*Envisioning the Future of Cooperation on Common Rivers in South Asia: A Cooperative Security Approach by Bangladesh and India to the Tipaimukh Dam*', 42:1 Water International (2017) 54–72.

Intelligence Community Assessment, '*Global Water Security*', ICA 2012–08, U.S. Office of the Director of National Intelligence (2 February 2012); https://www.dni.gov/files/documents/Special%20Report_ICA%20Global%20Water%20Security.pdf.

Islam, M. F., *Water Use and Poverty Reduction* (Springer, 2016).

Iyer, R. R., '*Hydro-Diplomacy for Hydro-Harmony*', in G. Pangare (ed.), *Hydro Diplomacy. Sharing Water Across Borders* (New Delhi: Academic Foundation, 2014) 75–84.

Iyer, R. R., '*Ganga Waters: Dispute and Resolution*,' paper prepared for the Water and Conflict in Asia Seminar, Asia-Pacific Center for Security Studies, Honolulu, Hawaii (17 September 1999).

Iyer, R. R., *Water: Perspectives, Issues, Concerns* (New Delhi: SAGE Publications; Strategic Foresight Group, 2013).

John, T., *'How China Could Weaponize Water'*, Time Magazine (3 October 2017), http://time.com/4951207/how-china-could-weaponize-water/.

Johnson, L., *'Advocacy Strategies for Promoting Greater Consideration of Climate Change and Human Rights in Development Activities: The Case of the West Seti Hydroelectric Project in Nepal'*, 27: 2 Pace Environmental Law Review (2010).

Kadurugamuwa, N., *Sharing of Trans-Boundary River Waters in South Asia; Geopolitics and Beyond* (2014).

Kamal, A., 'An Overview of the Seminar on Water Security', Margalla Papers, Special Edition, Vol. XV, No. 1, *National Defence University* (2011) ii–viii, http://www.ndu.edu.pk/issra/issra_pub/articles/margalla-paper/Margalla-Papers-SE-2011/Margalla-Papers-2011-Special-Edition.pdf.

Kapoor, D. K., *International Law and Human Rights* (India: Central Law Agency, 14th ed. 2002).

Keetelar, J. C., *Transboundary Water Issues in South Asia* (MSc Thesis, Erasmus University Rotterdam, International Public Management & Policy, August 2017).

Khalid, A. R. M., *'The Interlinking of Rivers Project in India and International Water Law: An Overview'*, 3:2 Chinese Journal of International Law (2004) 553–570.

Kibria, Z., & R. Laifungbam (eds.), *Tipaimukh Hydroelectric Multipurpose Project: Dam or Damage?* (Dhaka: BanglaPraxis & CORE, 2003).

Kirmani, S. S., *'Water, Peace and Conflict Management: The Experience of the Indus and Mekong River Basins'*, 15:4 Water International (1990) 200–205.

Kirmani, S., & G. Le Moigne, *'Fostering Riparian Cooperation in International River Basins, The World Bank at its Best in Development Diplomacy'*, Technical Paper No. 335, *World Bank* (Washington, DC, 1997).

Ku, J., *'China and the Future of International Adjudication'*, 27 Maryland Journal of International Law (2012) 154–173.

Kuokkanen, T., *'Water Security and International Law'*, PER/PELJ 2017 (20), http://www.scielo.org.za/pdf/pelj/v20n1/08.pdf.

Lamballe, A., *L'Eau en Asie du Sud. Confrontation ou Coopération?* (Harmattan, 2009).

Leb, C., *Cooperation in the Law of Transboundary Water Resources* (Cambridge: Cambridge University Press, 2013).

Leb, C., & P. Wouters, *'The Water Security Paradox and International Law: Securitization as an Obstacle to Achieving Water Security and The Role of Law in Desecuritizing the World's Most Precious Resources'*, in B. Lankford et al. (eds.), *Water Security: Principles, Perspectives, and Practices* (Abingdon and New York: Routledge, 2013).

Lipper, J., *'Equitable Utilization'*, in A. H. Garretson et al. (eds.), *The Law of International Drainage Basins* (Dobbs Ferry, NY: Oceana Publications, 1967) 15–88.

Liu, Y., *'Transboundary Water Cooperation on the Yarlung Zangbo/Brahmaputra—A Legal Analysis of Riparian State Practice'*, 40:2 Water International (2015) 354–374.

Magsig, B-O. *International Water Law and the Quest for Common Security* (London: Routledge, 2015).

Malla, K. B., *The Legal Regime of International Watercourse Progress and Paradigms Regarding Uses and Environmental Protection* (Ph.D. dissertation, Stockholm University, Faculty of Law, 2005).

Mason, E. S., & R. E. Asher, *The World Bank Since Bretton Woods* (Washington, DC: Brookings Institution, 1973).

McCaffrey, Stephen, '*The Codification of Universal Norms: A Means to Promote Cooperation and Equity?*', in L. Boisson de Chazournes et al. (eds.), *International Law and Freshwater: The Multiple Challenges* (Cheltenham: Edward Elgar, 2013) 125–139.

McCaffrey, S. C., *The Law of International Watercourses* (2nd ed., Oxford: Oxford University Press, 2007).

McCaffrey, S. C., *The Law of International Watercourses: Non-Navigational Uses* (Oxford: Oxford University Press, 2001).

McCaffrey, S. C., '*Watercourses Convention: The Convention Enters into Force*', 44:4 Environmental Policy and Law (2014) 351–356.

McCaffrey, S. C., '*Water, Politics and International Law*', in P. H. Gleick (ed.), *Water in Crisis: A Guide to the World's Fresh Water Resources* (Oxford: Oxford University Press, 1993) 92–104.

Mehta, J. S., '*Politics of Riparian Relations. Sustaining Development and Peace*', in B. G. Verghese & R. R. Iyer (eds.), *Harnessing the Eastern Himalayan Rivers: Regional Cooperation in South Asia* (New Delhi: Konark, 1994) 159–172.

Mekonnen, D. Z., '*The Nile Basin Cooperative Framework Agreement Negotiations and the Adoption of a "Water Security" Paradigm: Flight into Obscurity or a Logical Cul-de-sac?*', 21:2 European Journal of International Law (2010) 421–440.

Mirchandani, M., '*The Teesta Water Dispute: Geopolitics, Myth and Economics*', ORF Special Report No. 25, Observer Research Foundation (New Delhi, 21 September 2016).

Mustafa K., '*India Completes Kishenganga Project with Faulty Design*', The News International (Karachi) (28 November 2017).

Nesa, M., *A Step Toward Solving the South Asian Water Crisis*, Georgetown Journal of International Affairs (25 May 2015).

Nickum, E. J., '*The Upstream Superpower: China's International Rivers*', in O. Varis et al. (eds.), *Management of Transboundary Rivers and Lakes* (Berlin and Heidelberg: Springer, 2008) 227–244.

Nishat, A., '*A Review of the Institutional Framework for Management of Water Resources in the Ganges-Brahmaputra-Meghna System*', in G. Pangare (ed.), *Hydro Diplomacy: Sharing Water Across Borders* (New Delhi: Academic Foundation, 2014) 109–116.

Organisation for Economic Co-operation and Development, *Water Security for Better Lives*, OECD Studies on Water (Paris: OECD Publishing, 2013).

Pandey, P., '*Bangladesh, India, and Fifteen Years of Peace: Future Directions of the Ganges Treaty*', 54:4 Asian Survey (July/August 2014) 651–673.

Parsai, G., '*India, Pakistan Resolve Baglihar Dam Issue*', The Hindu (1 June 2010), http://www.thehindu.com/news/India-Pakistan-resolve-Baglihar-dam-issue/article16240199.ece.

Permanent Court of Arbitration, *In the Matter of the Indus Waters Kishenganga Arbitration* (Pakistan v. India), Final Award, 20 December 2013.

Pedersen, O. W., '*From Abundance to Indeterminacy: The Precautionary Principle and Its Two Camps of Custom*', 3:2 Transnational Environmental Law (2014) 323–339.

Pekkanen, S. M. et al. (eds.), *The Oxford Handbook of the International Relations of Asia* (Oxford: OUP, 2014).

Ping, G., & S. M. Davlin, '*Brahmaputra River*', Max Planck Encyclopedia of Public International Law, Max Planck Institute for Comparative Public Law and International Law, Heidelberg and Oxford University Press, 2010.

Prasai, S., & M. D. Surie, *Political Economy Analysis of the Teesta River Basin* (New Delhi: The Asia Foundation, 2013).

'*President Seeks SC View on SYL Row*', Rediff News (23 July2004), http://www.rediff.com/news/2004/jul/22syl.htm.

Price, G., & S. Mittra, *Water, Ecosystems and Energy in South Asia: Making Cross-border Collaboration Work*, Chatham House Research Paper (London: Royal Institute of International Affairs, June 2016).

Radosevich, G. E., '*The Mekong River Agreement: Lessons Learned*', in *Shared Water Systems and Transboundary Issues (With Special Emphasis on the Iberian Peninsula): Proceedings of the Conference held at Luso-American Development Foundation, Lisbon, Portugal, March 11 and 12, 1999* (Luso-American Development Foundation, 2000) 333–368.

Rahman, M. M., '*Hydropower Ambitions of South Asian Nations and China: Ganges and Brahmaputra Rivers Basins*', 4:1/2 International Journal of Sustainable Society (2012) 131–157.

Rahman, M. M., & O. Varis, '*Integrated Water Management of the Brahmaputra Basin: Perspectives and Hope for Regional Development*', 33:1 Natural Resources Forum (February 2009) 60–75.

Raman, D. D., *Governance of International Rivers: Threats, Gaps and Challenges* (Unpublished Ph.D. Thesis, University of Waikato, 2015).

Roul, A., '*India-China Hydro Diplomacy: Beyond Information Sharing MOUs*', Society for the Study of Peace and Conflict (22 March 2013), http://www.sspconline.org/opinion/IndiaChinaHydroDiplomacy_22032013.

Rashid, H. U., '*Indo-Bangladesh Framework Agreement*', The Daily Star (18 July 2012).

Rosegrant, M. W. et al., *World Water and Food to 2005: Dealing with Scarcity* (Washington, DC: International Food Policy Research Institute, 2002), https://reliefweb.int/

sites/reliefweb.int/files/resources/1B0BBA6D1080C010C1256C6E002E1D17-ifpri-water2025-16oct.pdf.

Sahai, I. M., '*Baglihar Decision—An End to the Dispute?*', 59:4 International Water Power and Dam Construction (2007).

Salman, S. M. A., '*Downstream Riparians Can also Harm Upstream Riparians: The Concept of Foreclosure of Future Uses*', 35 Water International (2010) 350–364; Chinese version, translated by D. Hu & Z. Tang, in G. Tan & L. Kong (eds.), *Symposium Proceedings for International Law and Practice of Transboundary Water Resources* (Beijing: China Social Sciences Academic Press, March 2012) 38–62.

Salman, S. M. A., '*Entry into Force of the UN Watercourses Convention: Why Should It Matter?*', 31:1 International Journal of Water Resources Development (2015) 4–16.

Salman, S. M. A., '*Inter-states Water Disputes in India: An Analysis of the Settlement Process*', 4:3 Water Policy (2002) 223–237.

Salman, S. M. A., '*Mediation of International Water Disputes—The Indus, the Jordan and the Nile Basins Interventions*', in L. Boisson de Chazournes et al. (eds.), *International Law and Freshwater: The Multiple Challenges* (Cheltenham: Edward Elgar, 2013) 360–405.

Salman, S. M. A., '*Sharing the Ganges Waters Between India and Bangladesh: An Analysis of the 1996 Treaty*', in S. M. A. Salman & L. Boisson de Chazournes, 'International Watercourses: Enhancing Cooperation and Managing Conflict', Technical Paper No. 414, *World Bank* (Washington, DC, 1998) 127–154.

Salman, S. M. A., '*The Baglihar Difference and its Resolution Process—A Triumph for the Indus Waters Treaty?*', 10 Water Policy (2008) 105–117.

Salman, S. M. A., '*The Changing Legal Contours of the Nile Basin—Do Agreements Really Matter?*', in S. McCaffrey et al. (eds.), *Research Handbook on International Water Law* (Cheltenham: Edward Elgar, 2018, forthcoming).

Salman, S. M. A., '*The Nile Basin Cooperative Framework Agreement: A Peacefully Unfolding African Spring?*', 38:1 Water International (2013) 17–29.

Salman, S. M. A., *The World Bank Policy for Projects on International Waterways: An Historical and Legal Analysis* (Leiden: Martinus Nijhoff Publishers, 2009; Washington, DC: The World Bank, 2009).

Salman, S. M. A., '*The United Nations Watercourses Convention Ten Years Later: Why Has its Entry into Force Proven Difficult?*', 32:1 Water International (2007) 1–15.

Salman, S. M. A., & K. Uprety, *Conflict and Cooperation on South Asia's International Rivers: A Legal Perspective* (The Hague: Kluwer Law International, 2003; Washington, DC: The World Bank, 2003).

Salman, S. M. A., & K. Uprety, '*Hydro-politics in South Asia: A Comparative Analysis of the Mahakali and Ganges Treaties*', 39 Natural Resources Journal (1999) 295–339.

Salman, S. M. A., & E. Obadia, '*The Indus Waters Treaty, the Baglihar Difference and ICSID Administration of the Proceedings*', 23: 2 News from International Centre for Settlement of Investment Disputes (2006) 1, 14–16.

Samaranayake, N. et al., *Water Resource Competition in the Brahmaputra River Basin* (Arlington, VA: CNA, 2016).

Seligman, D., *World's Major Rivers: An Introduction to International Water Law with Case Studies* (Las Vegas: Colorado River Commission of Nevada, 2004), http://crc.nv.Gov/docs/Worlds_Major_Rivers.pdf.

Shrestha, R. S., "Opinion," *West Seti Project. A Nepali Perspective* (September 2008).

Shrestha, S. et al., *Managing Water Resources under Climate Uncertainty* (Springer, 2015).

Siwakoti, G., *Transboundary River Basins in South Asia: Options for Conflict Resolution*, (Berkeley: International Rivers, 2011), https://www.internationalrivers.org/sites/default/files/attached-files/transboundaryriverbasins.pdf.

Smith P. J. & Lt. Col. C. H. Gross, *Water and Conflict in Asia?* (Honolulu, HI: Asia-Pacific Center for Security Studies 17 September 1999).

South Asia Team, '*Bhutan Rivers Watch*', International Rivers (16 June 2015), https://www.internationalrivers.org/resources/9059.

Subramanian, A., et al., '*Understanding and Overcoming Risks to Cooperation along Transboundary Rivers*', 16 Water Policy (2014) 824–843.

Surie, M., & S. Prasai, *Strengthening Transparency and Access to Information on Transboundary Rivers in South Asia* (New Delhi: The Asia Foundation, March 2015).

Swain, A., '*Reconciling Disputes and Treaties: Water Development and Management in Ganga Basin*', 6:1 Water Nepal (1998) 43–65.

Swain, A., '*South Asian Regional Council (SARC) and South Asian rivers: A Study in Water Conflict*', in M. Chatterji & B. M. Jain (eds.), *Conflict and Peace in South Asia (Contributions to Conflict Management, Peace Economics and Development)* (Bingley, UK: Emerald Group, 2008) 269–283.

Tarlock, A. D., '*Water Security, Fear Mitigation and International Water Law*', 31(3) Hamlin Law Review (2008) 703–728.

Tariq, S. M., *Pakistan-India Relations: Implementation of Indus Waters Treaty: A Pakistani Narrative*, background paper published by Pakistan Institute of Legislative Development and Transparency, Islamabad (December 2010).

Thapa, A. B., '*The Gandaki River Treaty*', 21 Spotlight (2002) 9–10.

Thatte, C. D., '*Indus Waters and the 1960 Treaty Between India and Pakistan*', in O. Varis et al. (eds.), *Management of Transboundary Rivers and Lakes* (Berlin and Heidelberg: Springer, 2008) 165–206.

Thomas, K. A., '*The River-border Complex: A Border-integrated Approach to Transboundary River Governance Illustrated by the Ganges River and Indo Bangladeshi Border*', 42:1 Water International (2017) 34–50.

Tignino, M., '*Le Fleuve Indus Et Ses Usages: L'arbitrage Relatif Aux Eaux Du Fleuve Kishenganga*', LX Annuaire Français de droit International (2014) 519–542.

Tiwari, R., '*Tulbul Project: India-Pak Talks Today*', The Indian Express, 11 May 2011, http://archive.indianexpress.com/news/tulbul-project-indiapak-talks-today/788727/.

United Nations Environment Programme, *Atlas of International Freshwater Agreements* (2002), http://wedocs.unep.org/handle/20.500.11822/8182.

Upreti, T., *International Watercourses Law and Its Application in South Asia* (Kathmandu: Pairavi Publishers, 2006).

Uprety, K., '*Nepal's West Seti Project Imbroglio: The Supreme Court Speaks*', 2 Beijing Law Review (2011) 17–24.

Uprety, K., '*Specially Invited Opinions and Research Report of the International Water Law Project: Global Perspectives on the Entry into Force of the UN Watercourses Convention 2014: Part One*', Gabriel Eckstein (Editor), 16 Water Policy (2014) 1198–1217.

Uprety, K., '*South Asian Water Treaty Practice: An Overview*', in S. McCaffrey et al. (eds.), *Research Handbook on International Water Law* (Cheltenham: Edward Elgar Publishers, 2018, forthcoming), Chapter 25.

Uprety, K., '*The Kishenganga Arbitration: Reviving the Indus Treaty and Managing Transboundary Hydropolitics*', 14 Chinese Journal of International Law (2015) 497–543.

Uprety, K., & S. M. A. Salman, '*Legal Aspects of Sharing and Management of Transboundary Waters in South Asia: Preventing Conflicts and Promoting Cooperation*', 56 Hydrological Science Journal (2011) 641–661.

Vasudha Foundation, *A Study of the India-Bhutan Energy Cooperation Agreements and the Implementation of Hydropower Projects in Bhutan* (New Delhi, 2016).

Verghese, B. G., '*The Indo-Bhutan, Indo-Nepal Dialogues*', in B. G. Verghese & R. R. Iyer (eds.), *Harnessing the Eastern Himalayan Rivers: Regional Cooperation in South Asia* (New Delhi: Konark Publishers, 1993) 199–211.

Verghese, B. G., & R. R. Iyer (eds.), *Harnessing the Eastern Himalayan Rivers: Regional Cooperation in South Asia* (New Delhi: Konark Publishers, 1993).

Vivekanandan, J., & S. Nair, '*Climate Change and Water: Examining the Interlinkages*' in D. Michel & A. Pandya, (eds.), *Troubled Waters: Climate Change, Hydropolitics, and Transboundary Resources* (Washington, DC: The Henry L. Stimson Center, 2009) 1–14.

Wang, T., '*International Law in China: Historical and Contemporary Perspectives*', 221 Recueil des Cours: Collected Courses of the Hague Academy of International Law (1990) 195–369.

Wheeler, W., '*The Water's Edge*', GOOD Magazine (13 July 2009).

Wirsing, R. G., & C. Jasparro, '*River Rivalry: Water Disputes, Resource Insecurity and Diplomatic Deadlock in South Asia*', 9 Water Policy (2007) 231–251.

Wolf, A. T., & J. T. Newton, *Case Study of Transboundary Dispute Resolution: the Indus Waters Treaty*, available at: https://www.researchgate.net/publication/251497725_Case_Study_of_Transboundary_Dispute_Resolution_the_Indus_Water_Treaty.

World Bank, '*World Bank Urges Mediation for India, Pakistan over Indus*', Press Release (10 November 2016), http://www.worldbank.org/en/news/press-release/2016/11/10/world-bank-urges-mediation-for-india-pakistan-over-indus.

World Bank, '*World Bank Declares Pause to Protect Indus Waters Treaty*', Press Release, 12 December 2016, http://www.worldbank.org/en/news/press-release/2016/12/12/world-bank-declares-pause-protect-indus-water-treaty.

World Bank, *World Development Indicators* (Washington, DC, 2017), https://data.worldbank.org/data-catalog/world-development-indicators.

'*World Bank Asks India, Pakistan To Agree to Mediation on Indus Waters Treaty*', The Economic Times (11 November 2016).

'*World Bank Halts Parallel Processes on India-Pakistan Hydel Projects*', The Economic Times (14 December 2016).

Wouters, P., '*Commentary, Considering China's approach to the UN Watercourses Convention—Time to revisit?*', International Water Law Project, https://www.internationalwaterlaw.org/blog/2014/07/28/professor-patricia-wouters-considering-chinas-approach-to-the-un-watercourses-convention-time-to-revisit/.

Wouters, P., 'International Law: Facilitating Transboundary Water Cooperation', TEC Background Papers No. 17, *Global Water Partnership* (Stockholm, 2013).

Wouters, P., & H. Chen, '*China's "Soft-path" to Transboundary Water Cooperation Examined in the Light of Two UN Global Water Conventions: Exploring the "Chinese way"*', 22 Journal of Water Law (2013) 229–247.

Wouters, P. et al., '*Water Security, Hydrosolidarity, and International Law: A River Runs Through It*', Yearbook of International Environmental Law (2009) 97–135.

Wuthnow, J., '*Water Power, Water Worries: China's Goals and Challenges as the Brahmaputra's Uppermost Riparian*', in N. Samaranayake et al., *Water Resource Competition in the Brahmaputra River Basin: China, India and Bangladesh* (Arlington, VA: CNA, May 2016).

Yaqoob, A., '*International River Waters in South Asia: Source of Conflict or Cooperation?*' (Islamabad: Pakistan Institute of Regional Studies, date unknown).

Zafar, A. & R. G. Wirsing (eds.), '*Imagining Industan: Overcoming Water Insecurity in the Indus Basin*' (Springer, 2017).

Zeitoun, M. et al., '*Transboundary Water Interaction II: The Influence of "Soft" Power*', 11:2 International Environmental Agreements: Politics, Law and Economics (2011) 159–278.

www.ingramcontent.com/pod-product-compliance
Lightning Source LLC
Chambersburg PA
CBHW031329230926
51848CB00001B/157
9789004385047